CAREERS IN DEMAND
FOR HIGH SCHOOL GRADUATES

Health Care & Science

Daniel Lewis

MASON CREST

Mason Crest
450 Parkway Drive, Suite D
Broomall, PA 19008
www.masoncrest.com

Printed in the United States of America
First printing
9 8 7 6 5 4 3 2 1

Series ISBN: 978-1-4222-4132-5
Hardcover ISBN: 978-1-4222-4137-0

Library of Congress Cataloging-in-Publication Data is available on file.

Developed and Produced by Print Matters Productions, Inc.
(www.printmattersinc.com)
Cover and Interior Design by Lori S Malkin Design, LLC

CAREERS IN DEMAND FOR HIGH SCHOOL GRADUATES

Agriculture, Food & Natural Resources

Armed Forces

Computers, Communications & the Arts

Construction & Trades

Fitness, Personal Care Services & Education

Health Care & Science

Hospitality & Human Services

Public Safety & Law

Sales, Marketing & Finance

Transportation & Manufacturing

KEY ICONS TO LOOK FOR:

 Words to understand: These words with their easy-to-understand definitions will increase the reader's understanding of the text while building vocabulary skills.

 Sidebars: This boxed material within the main text allows readers to build knowledge, gain insights, explore possibilities, and broaden their perspectives by weaving together additional information to provide realistic and holistic perspectives.

 Educational Videos: Readers can view videos by scanning our QR codes, providing them with additional educational content to supplement the text. Examples include news coverage, moments in history, speeches, iconic sports moments and much more!

 Text-dependent Questions: These questions send the reader back to the text for more careful attention to the evidence presented there.

 Research projects: Readers are pointed toward areas of further inquiry connected to each chapter. Suggestions are provided for projects that encourage deeper research and analysis.

CONTENTS

INTRODUCTION...6

Chapter 1: Occupational Therapist Aide/Physical Therapist Aide......13

Chapter 2: Dental Assistant 25

Chapter 3: Dispensing Optician 37

Chapter 4: Medical Receptionist... 49

Chapter 5: Veterinary Assistant/Laboratory Animal Caretaker 61

Chapter 6: Emergency Medical Technician/Paramedic 73

Chapter 7: Dialysis Technician.. 87

Chapter 8: Nursing Assistant 99

INDEX... 111

PHOTO CREDITS...112

Young people who choose a career path in health care often do so for altruistic reasons: Quite simply, they want to help others. Whether it's an emergency worker rushing to help an accident victim, or a dental assistant calming a nervous patient, health care workers take great satisfaction in knowing they make a difference in people's lives.

As the largest industry in the United States, the health care sector provides more than 19 million jobs. Health care jobs are especially plentiful in large states, such as California, New York, Florida, Texas, and Pennsylvania. For high school graduates, the health field can be a land of opportunity. In many cases, you can learn the required skills on the job. For more complex jobs, you may need to enroll in a specialized training program at a community college, trade school, or technical school. But unlike a degree program, the training for these positions can often be completed in just a few months. Plus, once you start working in health care, many employers will pay for additional training, allowing you to continue advancing in your career.

More important, the job outlook for health care workers looks promising in the coming years. According to Bureau of Labor Statistics' projections, employment in the health care sector is expected to increase by an astounding 19 percent between now and 2024—far faster than average. In fact, 12 of the 20 fastest-growing occupations will be in health-related fields. Specifically, employment opportunities are projected to increase by about

- 43 percent for occupational therapy assistants

- 41 percent for physical therapist assistants

- 39 percent for physical therapist aides

- 38 percent for home health aides

- 35 percent for nurse practitioners

- 34 percent for physical therapists

- 33 percent for ambulance drivers

- 31 percent for occupational therapy aides

- 30 percent for physician's assistants

- 29 percent for genetic counselors

- 29 percent for audiologists

- 27 percent for hearing aid specialists

Credit the aging population for much of the expected boom in medical careers. As people grow older, they typically require more care, thus creating a demand for health workers. Also, advances in medical technology have generated new positions for health care specialists who help identify and treat conditions that used to be untreatable. Plus, pressures to contain medical costs will produce new opportunities for support workers, such as dental assistants, occupational therapy aides, physical therapy aides, and pharmacy technicians. Workers in these support positions play a vital role in keeping our health care system running. More important, many of these jobs are open to high school graduates with a willingness to learn new skills.

One advantage of entering a field where employers are scrambling to fill key positions is that you can often negotiate valuable fringe benefits. Many health care providers, for example, reimburse employees who continue their educational training, while others provide family-friendly benefits, such as child care services and flexible schedules.

In this volume, you'll learn about the many rewarding career opportunities for high school graduates. The training requirements will vary, depending on the job and the employer. In some dental offices, for example, you may be able to start working right out of high school, and you will receive your training on the job. For more complex jobs, such as that of an emergency medical technician (EMT) or a dialysis technician, you'll need to enroll in specialized courses to become certified in your field. However, just because these courses focus just on the skills needed to do a specific job there's no need to put your life on hold. In many cases, the required training can be completed within just a few months.

While the job descriptions may vary, workers in health care all share one common goal: improving the health of their patients. Depending on the job title, the care provided may be dramatic, such as when a paramedic performs lifesaving cardiopulmonary resuscitation (CPR) on an accident victim. The care can also be given indirectly, such as when a medical receptionist fast-tracks paperwork so a worried patient can schedule a biopsy to screen for cancer sooner rather than later.

No matter what their job titles are, though, providers must be able to work together as a team. An EMT needs to communicate with his or her supervising emergency room doctor while treating a patient at an accident scene. A pharmacy technician must share information with doctors, nurses, and insurance specialists to ensure that patients get the medicine they need. Similarly, a medical technician must work in concert with medical technologists and doctors to analyze a patient's blood work.

Blood and Guts

When people think of the medical profession, they often visualize dramatic scenes from popular TV shows, such as *House* and *Grey's Anatomy*. For those who crave the excitement of such lifesaving work, the health field offers rewarding opportunities. An EMT has to know how to keep an accident victim from bleeding to death on the way to the emergency room.

Of course, not everyone has the disposition needed to deal with life-and-death situations, not to mention the sight of blood and open wounds. Luckily, not all health careers require a strong stomach: A medical receptionist spends much of his or her day behind a counter, greeting patients.

Other health care professionals work as therapists who help patients achieve specific goals. A physical therapist aide, for instance, helps a physical therapist teach patients to perform exercises that improve their ability to perform basic tasks, such as walking and standing.

Some professionals in this field also work in sales. A dispensing optician doesn't just help fit a customer with prescription glasses. He or she also sells them. Likewise, pharmacy technicians help out at the register, ringing up prescriptions and other drugstore goods. Some health care workers don't actually take care of people: veterinary assistants tend to dogs, cats, horses, and other animals.

As you would expect, most health care employees work inside medical facilities, such as doctors' offices, medical centers, and hospitals. There are exceptions, however. An EMT may need to work outdoors while providing emergency treatment to someone at an accident scene. Dialysis technicians and nursing aides sometimes provide care in patients' homes.

We could include only a sampling of health careers in this volume. Others you might want to explore include medical transcriptionist, respiratory therapist, cardiology technician, licensed practical nurse, and radiology technician.

Even though the job descriptions for the different health careers vary, all require some common skills. Whether you're a medical receptionist dealing with nervous patients or a dialysis technician setting up the machinery, you need to be a careful, conscientious worker who can be counted on to worry about the details. You also need to be a good communicator who can share vital medical information with other colleagues, the patients, and the patients' families.

Most important, you need to be a special kind of person who can be compassionate, yet not become so involved in a patient's well-being that you let your emotions affect your health and good judgment.

Get Started Now

While in high school, you can take steps that can help prepare you for a career in this field. For starters, enrolling in science, math, and communications classes will help you gain the skills needed to talk knowledgeably with medical professionals, to accurately calculate prescriptions, and to communicate clearly with patients.

Now is also a good time to volunteer or seek part-time work in a medical setting. Even if you can only work a few hours on the weekends or a couple of months during the summer, the time you spend answering phones in a medical clinic, helping out at a vet clinic, or volunteering in a nursing home will give you a competitive edge. Not only will you gain valuable work experience in your field but the professional contacts you make while working can often help you find a permanent position after you finish high school.

Is a Health Care Career Right for You?

Ask yourself the following questions to see if the careers in this book might be right for you.

- Do I enjoy helping others?

- Can I handle pressure?

- Am I a problem solver?

- Am I a team player who can take direction from others?

- Am I a conscientious worker?

- Am I good with details?

- Do I have solid math skills?

- Am I emotionally stable enough to handle life-and-death situations?

- If I want to provide patient care, can I handle the sight of blood and other bodily fluids?

- Am I dependable? (I've only missed very few days of school or work.)

- Can I get along with different personalities?

- Do I like variety in my work?

- Do I enjoy science?

- Am I interested in how the body works?

- Am I a quick thinker?

- Will I be flexible about my work schedules? (Am I willing to work weekends or nights?)

  If you answered yes to most of these, then a health care career might be for you.

Learn the Skills

When people think about the medical profession, many mistakenly assume that most jobs require years of advanced training. And while it's certainly true that doctors, dentists, and similar professionals require advanced degrees, many rewarding health care careers are available to high school graduates. In fact, a high school diploma is the highest educational milestone for more than half of the workers in nursing homes and residential care facilities, and for more than a quarter of all hospital workers.

Of course, some jobs of interest to high school graduates do require specialized training. A pharmacy technician must learn how to accurately fill prescriptions, and an EMT must know how to perform CPR. But, unlike college degree programs where you take a bit of everything, the training for these positions focuses on what you need to know to perform a specific job, and so the courses can often be completed quickly. Better yet, some employers provide on-the-job training and even pay for you to take courses at community colleges, technical schools, and trade schools. Hospitals and other large employers are often willing to pay for additional training, so you may even be able earn an associate's degree in your profession on your boss's dime. Depending on your interests, you can enroll in classes that lead to certificates in specialties such as emergency medicine, dialysis, and medical technology.

If your job requires training to become certified, be sure to look for a school that's accredited by professional associations in your field. Stay clear of so-called diploma mills that hand out worthless diplomas and certificates without teaching students the skills they need to work in their chosen professions. The best way to avoid such pitfalls is to enroll in accredited schools and programs. Some other sites that can help you make smart choices include the following:

- The Council for Higher Education Accreditation http://www.chea.org

- Commission on Accreditation of Allied Health Education Programs http://www.caahep.org

- Commission on Accreditation for Health Informatics and Information Management Education http://www.cahiim.org

- Accrediting Commission of the Career Schools and Colleges of Technology http://www.accsc.org

- Accrediting Bureau of Health Education Schools http://www.abhes.org

- American Veterinary Medical Association http://www.avma.org

- Commission on Dental Accreditation http://www.ada.org/en/coda

- Commission on Opticianry Accreditation http://www.coaccreditation.com

- Commission on Accreditation in Physical Therapy Education http://www.apta.org

- National Council of State Boards of Nursing http://www.ncsbn.org

- Accreditation Commission for Education Nursing http://www.acenursing.org/

- Committee on Accreditation for EMS Professionals http://www.coaemsp.org

◀ Emergency medical technicians (EMTs) are always on call for urgent care. If you enjoy a fast-paced work environment, this may be the job for you!

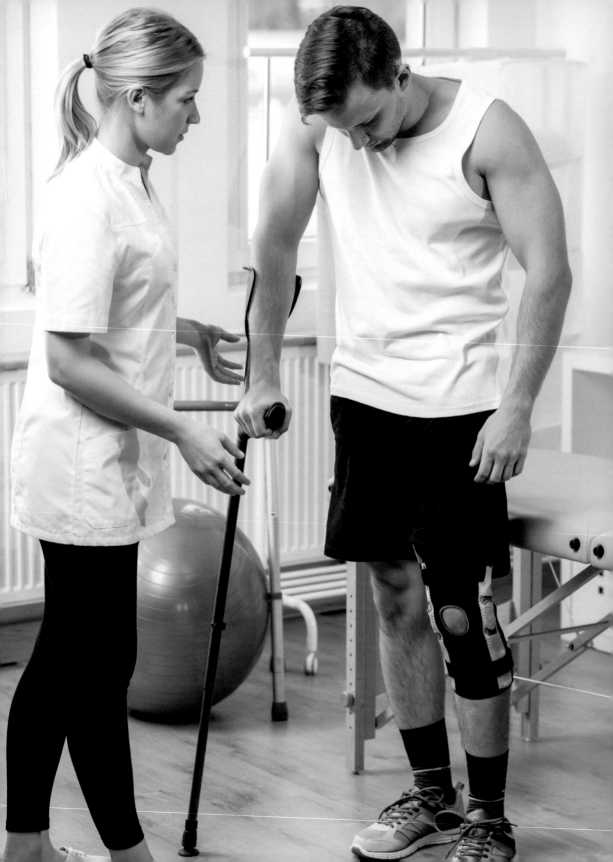

Occupational Therapist Aide/Physical Therapist Aide

1

Give emotional support to those in need.
Help injured people relearn physical skills.
Handle administrative work.

WORDS TO UNDERSTAND

clerical: refers to routine office tasks, such as typing, filing, or filling out paperwork.

daunting: difficult or intimidating.

empathetic: describes someone with the ability to understand the feelings of others.

Buttoning a shirt. Climbing the stairs. Writing a note. These are essential tasks that most of us take for granted. Yet for a child with poor fine motor skills, or a stroke victim who can't remember how to walk, performing such simple tasks can be **daunting**. Thanks to occupational and physical therapy programs, children and adults who need help learning, or in some cases relearning, such tasks can often show dramatic improvement.

As an occupational therapist aide or physical therapist aide, your job is to help therapists help their patients. You may, for example, assist

◀ A physical therapy aide helps a patient regain strength and mobility.

a physical therapy patient who is walking to a treatment area on crutches, or set up occupational therapy toys for a child with weak fine motor skills. As an aide, you set up patient appointments, file insurance claims, and order supplies. In addition to performing clerical duties, your supportive, upbeat attitude can help patient morale. If a patient is frustrated because his or her broken leg is taking a long time to heal or because he or she is having trouble grasping a toothbrush, you can often help that patient feel better simply by lending an understanding ear.

Is This Job Right for You?

To find out if being an occupational physical therapist aide or a physical therapist aide is for you, read each of the following questions and answer "Yes" or "No."

Yes	*No*	1. *Do you like working with people from many different backgrounds?*
Yes	*No*	2. *Are you physically fit?*
Yes	*No*	3. *Do you like helping people who can't always help themselves?*
Yes	*No*	4. *Are you **empathetic** with people who are in need?*
Yes	*No*	5. *Are you organized?*
Yes	*No*	6. *Can you handle tasks such as answering telephones, scheduling appointments, and ordering supplies?*
Yes	*No*	7. *Are you discreet? Do you understand the importance of honoring a patient's confidentiality?*
Yes	*No*	8. *Do you have a positive attitude and can you provide encouragement to others?*
Yes	*No*	9. *Do you follow directions well?*
Yes	*No*	10. *Are you dependable?*

If you answered "Yes" to most of these questions, you might consider a career as an occupational therapist aide or physical therapist aide. To find out more about these jobs, read on.

What's the Work Like?

Your main role as an occupational therapist aide or a physical therapist aide is to help occupational therapists and physical therapists do their jobs. In that role, you gather and prepare the materials and equipment needed for each patient's therapy session. If you work for an occupational therapist, the patient will receive therapy to help him or her master essential life skills, such as grasping a fork, tying shoes, and picking up coins. If the patient is too injured or disabled to walk to the treatment room unassisted, you may need to help him or her get there. You may, for example, lift a patient from a bed, provide assistance in the bathroom, or transport a patient in a wheelchair to the treatment room.

A physical therapist aide performs many of the same duties as an occupational therapist aide, only physical therapy tends to focus on

TALKING MONEY

Occupational therapist aides make a median annual salary of $28,330 with the top 10 percent making more than $51,180 a year, according to 2016 statistics from the U.S. Bureau of Labor Statistics. Physical therapist aides make a median annual salary of $25,680 with the top 10 percent making more than $38,340 per year. Those who advance to become therapy assistants earn significantly more—an average of $56,610 per year, according to the Bureau of Labor Statistics.

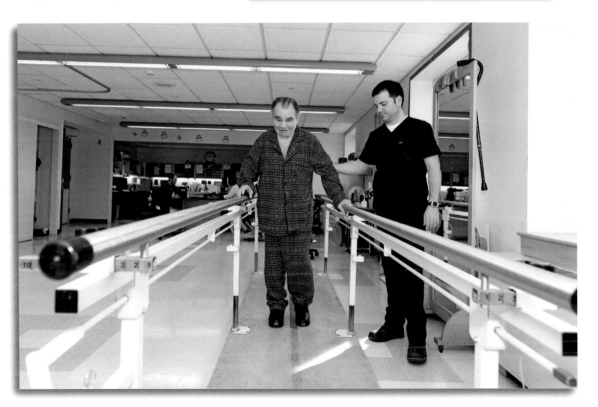

▲ A physical therapy aide assists a patient with gait therapy using parallel bars.

helping patients become more mobile and regain strength. During physical therapy, a stroke victim may work on learning to walk again; a child who has broken an arm may work on strengthening the muscles; or a baby with low muscle tone may work with a therapist to gain enough strength to eventually sit up without needing assistance.

Occupational therapist aides and physical therapist aides also carry out important **clerical** and administrative duties, from handling phone calls to scheduling appointments to filling out medical forms.

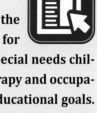

TALKING TRENDS

An aging population will fuel the rapidly increasing demand for workers in this field, as will special needs children who require physical therapy and occupational therapy to meet their educational goals. Opportunities are expected to grow by about 41 percent—much faster than the average for all occupations—through 2024.

Who's Hiring?

- Hospitals

- Nursing homes

- Senior citizen community centers

- School districts

- Home health care services

- County and state government agencies

- Offices of occupational therapists and physical therapists

Where Are the Jobs?

Occupational therapist aides and physical therapist aides work wherever occupational therapists and physical therapists work. You may, for example, help an occupational therapist or physical therapist in a private office (about 36 percent of aide jobs) or in a hospital

▲ An occupational therapist aide helps a young girl to improve her fine motor skills.

(28 percent of these jobs), nursing home (15 percent), social assistance organization (6 percent) or school (4 percent). About 55 percent of physical therapist aides work in the offices of physical therapists. They also find positions in hospitals (21 percent), doctors' offices (8 percent), nursing homes (6 percent), or for the government (3 percent). Because patients can't always come in during regular business hours throughout the week, some therapists and their aides work nights and weekends.

A Typical Day

Here are the highlights for a typical day for an occupational therapist aide.

Set up the treatment area. Gather and arrange the therapy tools that the therapists will need for the sessions they have planned for the day. Depending on a patient's physical condition, you may need to help move him or her to the treatment area.

NOTES FROM THE FIELD

Occupational therapist aide, *West Haverstraw, New York*

Q: *How did you get your job?*

A: I got my job by seniority. When I started working here a few years ago, I was a nurse's aide on the head injury unit. When an opening occurred to work as an occupational therapist aide, I put in for it.

Q: *What do you like best about your job?*

A: You're helping patients learn activities needed for daily living. You're helping them learn to dress. You're helping them learn activities like putting on a shirt, brushing their teeth, and combing their hair.

Because you're helping someone and you're teaching them something so they can be independent, it's very rewarding to see them come from one level and go to another. Seeing an improvement in a patient makes you feel good.

Q: *What's the most challenging part of your job?*

A: When patients don't understand you. Sometimes patients can't follow the directions and you don't have the right words to explain it.

Q: *What are the keys to success to being an occupational therapist aide?*

A: Listen to the occupational therapist. Be very observant. Never be afraid to ask questions if you don't understand something.

Keep the office going. In some offices, you help out at the front desk. You greet patients, maintain a calendar of patient appointments, and make reminder phone calls. You also check supplies periodically and order new items as needed.

Handle paperwork. You file insurance claims. You type and mail reports on a patient's progress to various parties, such as a child's school or a patient's primary physician.

Support the therapist. The therapist may ask you to take notes during a patient's therapy sessions. You might, for example, write down how often a patient is able to do a particular exercise, or how long it takes to perform a particular task. Under the direction of the therapist, you may practice basic skills with the patient, such as putting on clothes and brushing teeth.

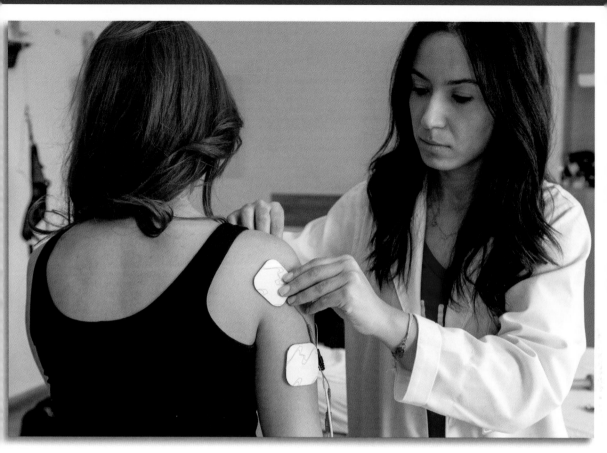

▲ Physical therapists often use transcutaneous electrical nerve stimulation (TENS). By making muscles contract, it increases a patient's range of motion and improves circulation. The physical therapy aide here is attaching electrodes to the injured area.

Start Preparing Now

- Take courses on health and administrative skills. Taking health courses that deal with medical terminology, anatomy, and physiology can also help prepare you to work in this field.

- Experience counts. Volunteering or working part time in an office, a health care clinic, or a therapist's office will provide you with valuable experience and contacts who may be able to help you find a permanent job once you finish your schooling.

- Help others. You can better decide if this work is for you by assisting others. If you know friends or family who are sick and injured, take some time to help them with their everyday activities.

Training and How to Get It

To be considered for a position as an occupational therapist aide or physical therapist aide, you generally need to have completed high school. While much of your training will be on the job, candidates with clerical and/or health care experience will have an edge in the job pool. Whether you volunteer at a medical clinic or work part time at a local office, you'll gain valuable skills that will impress prospective employers.

 See what it's like to be a physical therapy aide.

Learn the Lingo

Here are a few words and phrases you'll hear as an aide:

- **Sensory integration** Occupational therapists use this term to refer to a person's ability to take in information through the senses, such as touch, sound, smell, and sight. People with sensory difficulties often benefit from occupational therapy. An occupational therapist, for example, may provide therapy to help someone who is overly sensitive to sounds and touch.

- **OT** This is shorthand for "occupational therapy," as in, "The patient receives OT three times a week."

- **PT** Likewise, the phrase "physical therapy" is commonly shortened to PT.

Finding a Job

Prepare a résumé that showcases your skills, especially those that will help you do a good job as an occupational therapist aide or physical therapist aide. Be sure to include references (teachers, former bosses, etc.) who can vouch for your work ethic and dependability.

Send your résumé to health care providers who provide occupational or physical therapy. Follow up with periodic phone calls so they know you're still interested. If an employer doesn't have an opening for a therapist aide, consider taking another entry-level job there. When an opening does occur, you'll already have your foot in the door.

▲ An occupational therapist aide leads a young girl in a game designed to engage her gross motor skills.

Tips for Success

- Be ready to juggle a variety of tasks. One moment, you'll be filing insurance paperwork and contacting patients about their visits. In the next moment, you'll be holding up a stroke victim, supporting the patient as he or she walks to the treatment area, or letting a frustrated mother vent about her child's difficulties learning to tie his or her shoes.

- Take advantage of volunteer opportunities. You can prepare yourself for a job in this field and see if the career is a good match for you by volunteering or taking part-time employment at a hospital. Ask specifically to work as an aide to a physical or occupational therapist.

Reality Check

Are you strong? Some patients aren't strong enough to walk to the treatment area, or even get out of bed. As a physical therapist aide or occupational therapist aide, you must have enough strength and agility to safely move a patient. Try to see if you can carry a friend across the room—if you can do this, you're at least physically prepared to embark on this career.

LEARN MORE ONLINE

AMERICAN OCCUPATIONAL THERAPY ASSOCIATION
The "Education & Careers" portion of this site offers special information for students interested in the field. http://www.aota.org

AMERICAN PHYSICAL THERAPY ASSOCIATION
This association is all about "the science of healing and the art of caring." All the latest news on the career is here, along with an education section and job bank. http://www.apta.org

Related Jobs to Consider

Dental assistant. As a dental assistant, you work in a dental office, typically commanding the front greeting desk. You handle the phones, greet patients, schedule patient visits, file insurance forms, and lend a hand to the dentists while they work on patients.

Pharmacy technician. You assist the pharmacist in preparing prescriptions. You also ring up orders, answer phones, and handle insurance claims.

How to Move Up

- Earn a two-year degree. You can have more responsibilities and earn more money by earning an associate's degree in your field. With the additional training, you'll be able to deliver more hands-on care to patients.

- Look for a medical records technician position. Medical record technicians make sure that patients' initial medical charts are complete; that all forms are completed, properly identified, and signed; and that all necessary information is in the computer. It's a perfect position to advance to after working as an aide.

TEXT-DEPENDENT QUESTIONS

1. *What are some examples of people who need physical therapy? Occupational therapy?*

2. *What is sensory integration?*

3. *How might you move up in this field?*

RESEARCH PROJECTS

1. *Because much of this job involves clerical duties, you can get a head start on your career by taking vocational education courses that teach office skills. If you are of legal age, get a part-time or summer job that involves basic office work; trying your hand at this sort of job will help you decide if you would be successful with the clerical aspects of therapy aides.*

2. *Offer to help an elderly relative or neighbor with daily tasks. Does he or she need help buying groceries, cleaning up, or getting bills paid and organized? Ask what you can do to assist—this is a great test to see if you have the patience required to be successful as a therapy aide.*

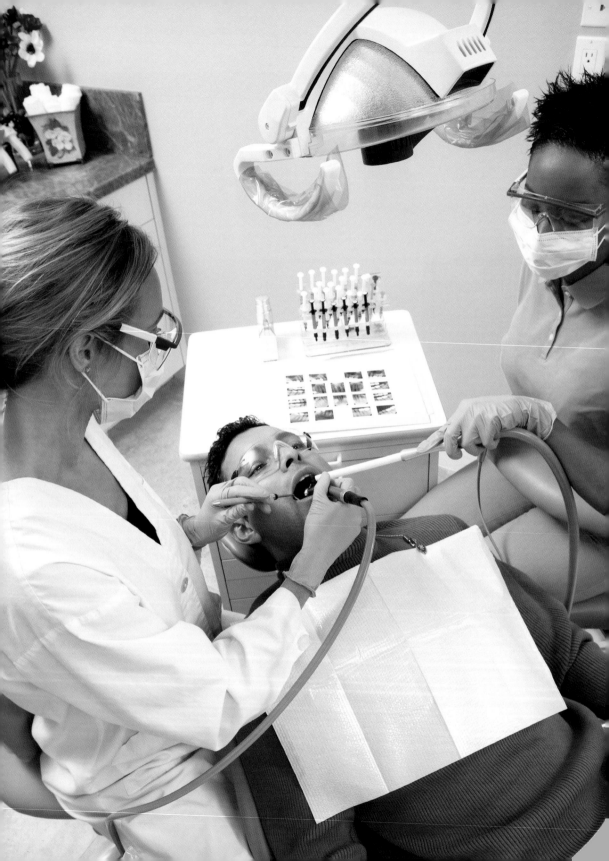

Dental Assistant

2

Provide essential support to dentists. Assist patients. Promote oral hygiene.

WORDS TO UNDERSTAND

ambience: the mood or atmosphere of a place.

sterilize: to make something completely free of all microorganisms.

sutures: stitches.

Smile! As a dental assistant, you'll have a chance to help others keep their teeth in good shape. Your main role will be to assist the dentist and help his or her office run smoothly. You'll offer patients advice on caring for their teeth. In some dental offices, you'll also assist the dentist while he or she works. You'll hand equipment to the dentist and hold suction tools and other devices in a patient's mouth. You'll prepare the dental instruments, take dental X-rays, and help remove **sutures**. Because dental health affects a patient's overall well-being, dental assistants take pride in knowing that they help keep a patient's teeth—and entire body—in good health.

◀ A dental assistant holds the suction tube while the hygienist cleans a patient's teeth.

Is This Job Right for You?

To find out if being a dental assistant is a good fit for you, read each of the following questions and answer "Yes" or "No."

Yes **No**	**1.**	*Do you have excellent eye–hand coordination?*
Yes **No**	**2.**	*Do you like helping others?*
Yes **No**	**3.**	*Do you have a reassuring, soothing manner?*
Yes **No**	**4.**	*Are you a careful worker who cares about the details?*
Yes **No**	**5.**	*Do you have strong fine motor skills?*
Yes **No**	**6.**	*Are you a good communicator who can share helpful information with others?*
Yes **No**	**7.**	*Are you a good listener?*
Yes **No**	**8.**	*Do you have good organizational skills?*
Yes **No**	**9.**	*Are you comfortable using a computer?*
Yes **No**	**10.**	*Can you follow directions well?*

If you answered "Yes" to most of these questions, consider a career as a dental assistant. To find out more about this job, read on.

What's the Work Like?

Dental assistants help care for patients in a dental office. They often work right alongside a dentist, handing him or her instruments, or holding a suction device in a patient's mouth. Tasks vary from office to office and are often dependent on an assistant's training. Some dental assistants make casts of the teeth, make temporary crowns, take dental X-rays, or remove sutures. Others run the office. They schedule appointments, handle payments, pay office bills, and

TALKING MONEY

The median wage for dental assistants is about $17.76 an hour, according to 2016 data from the U.S. Bureau of Labor Statistics. Annual earnings ranged widely, with the top 10 percent earning more than $52,000 and the bottom 10 percent earning less than $25,000. The majority of jobs are full time, but a not-insignificant number—almost one in three—are part-time positions.

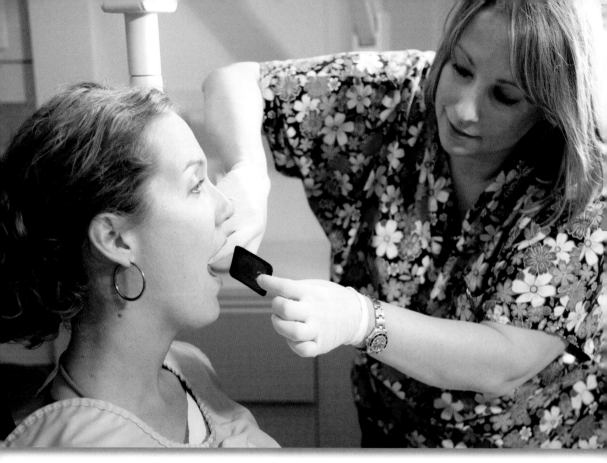

▲ A dental assistant positions X-ray film to image a patient's teeth. The lead apron or jacket over the patient limits radiation exposure during the X-ray.

order dental supplies. Many work part time and have flexible schedules that let them choose which days and hours they work. Some work in more than one dentist's office.

Who's Hiring?

- Individual dentist's office

- A group dental practice with more than one dentist

- Specialized practices, including orthodontics, periodontics, and pediatric dentistry

- Health clinics with dental services

Where Are the Jobs?

Dental assistants work in comfortable surroundings with air conditioning and a quiet, soothing **ambience** to keep patients at ease. Offices are very well lit because you have to see exactly what you're doing when performing dental work. You'll be in a very clean environment with sophisticated dental devices, including the reclining chair, drills, lights, and X-ray devices.

TALKING TRENDS

The demand for skilled dental assistants is expected to be strong, with the job growth exceeding that of other occupations, according to 2016 data from the Bureau of Labor Statistics. One reason? Not only are people living longer, but many more are keeping their teeth, fueling an increase in the need for dental care.

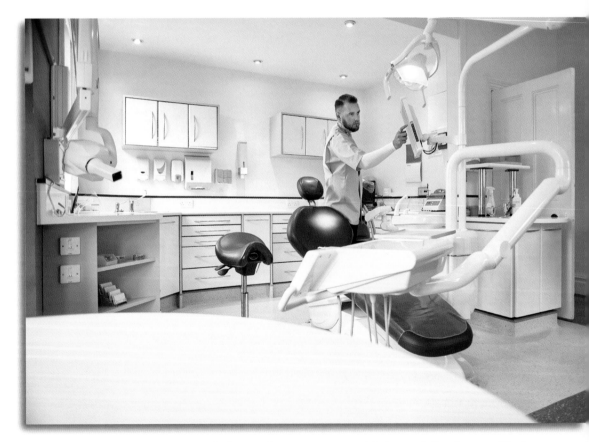

▲ A dental assistant preps an exam room before a patient enters to ensure it is clean and all tools are sterilized.

NOTES FROM THE FIELD

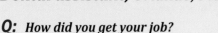

Dental assistant, *Orlando, Florida*

Q: *How did you get your job?*

A: My high school had dual-enrollment, so I was able to go to a dental assistant school while I was still in high school. The clinic needed people, so my teacher sent me over. After a month of interviewing and interviewing, they hired me.

Q: *What do you like best about your job?*

A: I think the best part of the job is helping people. I love it because we work for health centers that provide care to the homeless and to kids and to people who have been rejected at other places. We provide care to people who thought there was no hope. Part of my job is to go out and promote our service and let people know there's help out there.

Q: *What's the most challenging part of your job?*

A: The most challenging part of the job would be dealing with the patients, especially the ones who come in with an emergency. Having a tooth pain is something weird for the person it's happening to. They're desperate to stop the pain. It's very difficult to keep myself calm to calm them.

The emergency patients are my biggest challenge because we treat a lot of homeless people, and people going through drug rehabilitation, or with emotional problems. You just want to give them a good experience going to the dentist. Because they're afraid, we do whatever helps: We hold their hand. We talk to them.

Q: *What are the keys to success to being a dental assistant?*

A: As a dental assistant, you're not just doing what the doctor tells you. It's so much more than that. It's very important to have people skills. One of the main things we're dealing with is patients all day long. You have to have the patience to deal with all kinds of patients. You need to be knowledgeable about everything that's going on and keep updated on new things, new products and new findings.

A Typical Day

Here are the highlights of a typical workday as a dental assistant.

Do first things first. At the beginning of the day, you look over the day's appointments, check the patients' charts, and ready the supplies for the day.

Greet patients. When a patient arrives, you check the patient in. You also update any changes in a patient's dental insurance, mailing address, or phone numbers. You check with the patient to see if there are any changes in his or her medical status.

▲ Dental assistants often need to teach their patients—especially children—about good dental hygiene. Here, a dental assistant instructs a young patient how to brush his teeth properly.

Assist the dentist. You **sterilize** instruments and equipment and prepare trays of instruments for the dentist to use on patients.

Help with patient care. In some dental offices, you may be involved in patient care. You may, for example, take and develop X-rays of the teeth, assist a dentist while he or she puts in a crown, and hold suction devices in a patient's mouth during treatment.

Educate. You provide patients with tips on caring for their teeth and gums.

Do office work. During the day, you call patients to remind them about upcoming appointments. You file insurance claims for patients. You also keep track of the inventory and order any needed supplies.

Start Preparing Now

- Look for a vocational-education course or programs in health careers at your high school.
- You can get a jump on a career as a dental assistant in high school by taking related courses, such as biology, chemistry, and office management.

Training and How to Get It

Most states require dental assistants to be licensed or registered, but the training and testing requirements vary from state to state. Even though national certification is voluntary in some states, taking the time to pass certification exams administered by the Dental Assisting National Board (DANB) shows potential employers that you have mastered the skills needed to do the job and take your career seriously.

Students who enroll in dental assistant programs can often complete their training in less than a year's time, or they can opt to pursue a two-year degree. Students who want to be dental assistants can choose from hundreds of accredited programs. Dental assistant students receive instruction in classrooms and have opportunities to gain real-life experience in dental schools, clinics, and dental offices.

See what it's like to be a dental assistant.

Learn the Lingo

Here are a few words to know as a dental assistant:

- **Sealants** Dental sealants are a protective coating that is often applied to the biting surfaces on the back of children's teeth to keep cavities from forming.

- **Impression** In a dentist's office, an impression has nothing to do with impressing someone. When a dentist needs to make dentures, inlays, or plastic models of a patient's teeth, he or she makes an impression—a plastic imprint of the teeth and surrounding tissues—that hardens into a mold.

- **Abscess** A swollen area within the tissues that contains an accumulation of pus.

Finding a Job

Prepare a résumé that highlights your training and skills. Make sure you line up references (teachers, coaches, former bosses, etc.) who can vouch for your dependability, dedication, and any job-related skills. Send the résumé to dental offices and other facilities that employ dental assistants. Be sure to follow up with a phone call or two.

Reach out to professional dental associations, which often have local chapters and mentors who can put you in touch with the right people. If you are enrolled in a dental assisting program, your instructor or school placement office may also be able to help you find openings in your field.

Tips for Success

- Smile! And not just because you work in a dental office. As a dental assistant, you're often the first person a patient sees. If you're friendly, helpful, and empathetic, the patient is apt to view a visit to a dentist in a more positive light.

- Keep things neat. Equipment has to be organized, ready, and clean. Make sure dental tools are ready to go before each appointment.

Reality Check

Do you brush and floss? Regularly? If you're going to work in a dental office, you need to set a good example for the patients. After all, dental patients don't want to be greeted by a dental assistant with a piece of spinach stuck between his or her teeth.

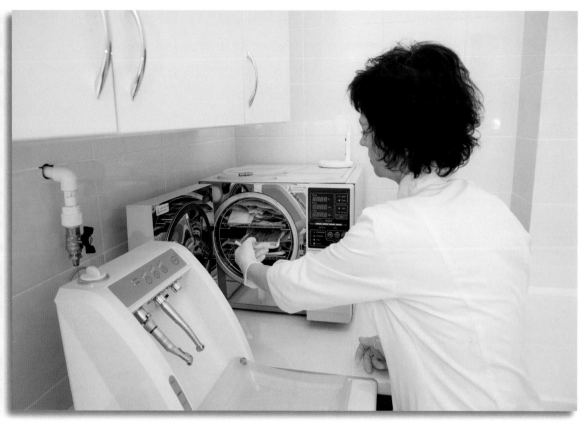

▲ A dental assistant places tools in a sterilizer to ensure their cleanliness for the next appointment.

Related Jobs to Consider

Phlebotomist. Phlebotomists collect and label blood. They may also deal with urine and other lab samples.

Licensed practical nurse (LPN). LPNs can administer most medications, change dressings, and perform other technical skills.

Clinical laboratory technician. If you enjoy doing lab experiments in science class, you might enjoy working as a clinical laboratory technician in a medical lab. As a clinical laboratory technician, you prepare lab specimens, perform manual tests on the specimens, and operate automated analyzers.

Pharmacy technician. Pharmacy technicians help pharmacists prepare prescriptions for patients.

How to Move Up

- Become a dental hygienist. You can gain the training needed to work as a dental hygienist in a two-year program at a community college. As a dental hygienist, you can clean a patient's teeth and help the dentist perform more complex procedures.

- Seek an office manager position. If you have strong organizational skills, you can work as an office manager in a large dental practice.

- Use your people skills. Dental assistants with strong people skills can work as instructors in dental assistant programs and as dental product sales representatives.

LEARN MORE ONLINE

ACADEMY OF GENERAL DENTISTRY
This group promotes excellence in oral health care. http://www.agd.org

AMERICAN DENTAL ASSISTANTS ASSOCIATION
This organization provides details on educational requirements, scholarships, and professional advice for dental assistants. http://www.adaausa.org/

AMERICAN DENTAL HYGIENISTS' ASSOCIATION
This is the professional association for hygienists. http://www.adha.org

AMERICAN DENTAL ASSOCIATION
View materials here for dentists. http://www.ada.org

DENTAL JOBS AT DENTAL WORKERS
Check out work opportunities at this site. http://www.dentalworkers.com

TEXT-DEPENDENT QUESTIONS

1. *What does a dental assistant do?*

2. *How do they get training?*

3. *What is a typical day like?*

4. *What are some related careers you might consider?*

RESEARCH PROJECTS

1. *Find out more about the past, present, and future of dentistry. Check out these books about the past:* **The Excruciating History of Dentistry** *by James Wynbrand,* **Dentistry: An Illustrated History** *by Malvin E. Ring. Look up articles about where the field is headed, such as "The Future of Dentistry" (http://www.dentaleconomics.com/articles/print/volume-95/issue-9/features/the-future-of-dentistry.html) and "Digital Dentistry" (http://www.dentaleconomics.com/articles/print/volume-101/issue-10/features/digital-dentistry-is-this-the-future-of-dentistry.html). You can also ask your librarian for suggestions.*

2. *Reach out to a local chapter of American Dental Assistant Association (search "American Dental Assistants Association" and your state). Doing so will help you find a mentor who can advise you on career choices. Your mentor may even be able to arrange for you to spend a day with a dental assistant, so you can see what a typical day is like.*

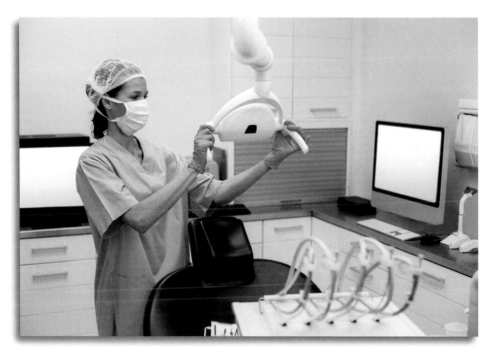

▲ Dental assistants are responsible for keeping equipment organized, ready, and clean before each patient.

Dispensing Optician

3

Learn the science of sight. Work with diverse customers. Help people see.

WORDS TO UNDERSTAND

apprentice: someone getting on-the-job training in a particular trade.
corrective: designed to adjust or repair something harmful.
focimeter: device used by opticians to verify prescriptions.

If you need new prescription glasses, a dispensing optician can help you find just the right pair. Commonly referred to as opticians, these skilled workers are licensed to adapt and fit **corrective** glasses based on a prescription written by an optometrist. Some opticians are also licensed to work with contact lenses.

When customers come in with prescriptions for eyeglasses, an optician helps them select frames that suit their face and personal style. An optician's main job is to make sure the customer's prescription is filled correctly. Seasoned opticians with fashion-savvy and good communication skills do much more. Consider the anxious child who needs his or her first pair of reading glasses. As a skilled optician, you will talk up the idea of glasses while helping the child find a cool-looking pair that will turn his or her worried frown into an "I-can't-wait to-show-off-my-new-glasses" grin.

◀ A dispensing optician helps customers choose the one pair of glasses that's right for them from among hundreds of styles.

Is This Job Right for You?

To find out if being a dispensing optician is a good fit for you, read each of the following questions and answer "Yes" or "No."

Yes	*No*	1. *Do you communicate well with others?*
Yes	*No*	2. *Do you have strong math skills?*
Yes	*No*	3. *Do you like helping other people?*
Yes	*No*	4. *Do you have a good sense of style?*
Yes	*No*	5. *Do you have patience?*
Yes	*No*	6. *Are you good with details?*
Yes	*No*	7. *Do you have strong fine-motor skills?*
Yes	*No*	8. *Are you tactful?*
Yes	*No*	9. *Do you have an interest in how the human body operates?*
Yes	*No*	10. *Can you work on your feet for long stretches at a time?*

If you answered "Yes" to most of these questions, consider a career as a dispensing optician. To find out more about this job, read on.

What's the Work Like?

As a dispensing optician, you help customers select glasses and frames that fit and flatter their face. To make sure the prescription is filled correctly, you measure the distance between the center of a customer's pupils and the distance between the ocular surface and the lens. If a customer doesn't have a new prescription, you can remake the eyeglasses from old prescription records or use a **focimeter** to record the eyeglass measurements of a current pair.

You then prepare a work order, so the technicians can make the lenses according to the correct specifications, and put them into the right frames. Once the glasses are ready, you make sure the lenses have been ground correctly and placed properly in the right frames. Then, when the customer comes in to pick up the glasses, you help him or her try on the new pair, and adjust the glasses until the fit is just right. Plus, you offer tips on how to wear and care for the new glasses.

TALKING MONEY

The median annual salary for dispensing opticians is about $35,530, according to 2016 data from the U.S. Bureau of Labor Statistics. The top earners in the field make more than $57,180 a year.

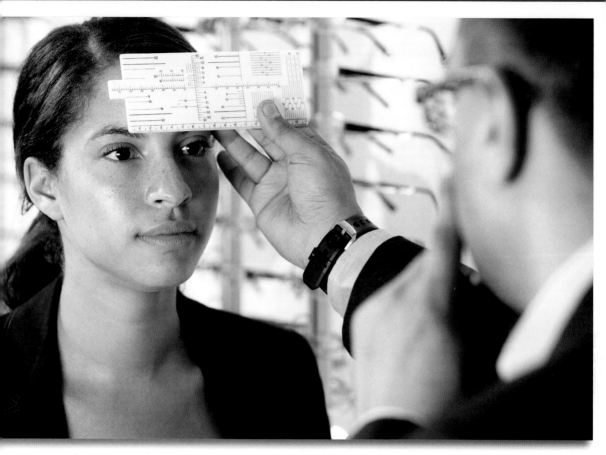

▲ An optician measures the distance between the center of a customer's pupils and the distance between the ocular surface and the lens to ensure that the eyeglasses will fit properly.

Some opticians are trained to fit customers with contact lenses. To fit the lenses, you measure the shape and size of the eye. You also help the customer select the best type of contact lens (hard, soft, disposable, etc.), and prepare a work order for the lenses.

Who's Hiring?

- Optical stores

- Medical offices and health clinics

- Optical shops inside department stores

- Optical shops in discount outlets

Where Are the Jobs?

Of the estimated 75,200 opticians who work in the United States, about 38 percent are employed in medical offices, including optometry offices. Another third work in health stores, optician stores, and other personal care stores. Some opticians work in department stores, warehouse clubs, and other large venues, while others run their own businesses.

Opticians' hours vary, depending on where they work. Those who work for large retailers, for example, sometimes work weekends and nights. Like many retail workers, opticians spend much of their day on their feet—so buy comfortable shoes if you're heading into this field.

A Typical Day

Here are the highlights of a typical day working as an optician.

Find the right glasses. You'll help customers select frames for their lenses that fit and accentuate their face in a positive, aesthetically pleasing way.

Take measurements. To make sure the prescription is filled correctly, you take specific eye measurements, such as the distance between the centers of a customer's pupils and the distance between the ocular surface and the lens.

Prepare the work order. You'll write up a work order with the required specs so a technician can make the lenses and put them in the right frame.

Check and adjust glasses. Once the glasses are ready, you make sure the lenses have been ground to the correct specifications. Using your hands or a pair of pliers, you bend or reshape the frames so they fit the patient's face comfortably without falling off.

Work with contact lenses. To fit a patient with contact lenses, you observe the patient's eyes, corneas, and lids while working with special instruments and microscopes. During follow-up visits, you teach the customer how to insert, remove, and care for the lenses, and make sure the fitting is correct.

Handle paperwork. You'll keep customer records, prepare work orders, and track payments, inventory, and sales.

▲ Children may feel uncomfortable wearing glasses. It is an optician's job to find the perfect pair of glasses that will make a child feel stylish and comfortable.

Start Preparing Now

- While in high school, be sure to take courses in math and physics.

- Flip through fashion magazines to stay abreast of fashion trends.

- Study (discreetly, of course) people's faces to see which eyewear styles work and which don't for people with different-shaped faces, hair color, and skin tones.

TALKING TRENDS

As the baby boomers continue to age, so do their eyes, creating a big demand for corrective glasses and lenses. Growing numbers of people with chronic illnesses that affect eyesight, such as diabetes, will also contribute to a predicted 24 percent increase in the number of dispensing opticians.

Training and How to Get It

You can pick up the skills you need as an **apprentice** in an optical shop (typically for two years), as a student enrolled in optician courses at a community college or tech school, or through a combination of the two. During your educational training, you'll learn how to adapt and fit corrective eyewear. You'll learn how to help patients select frames, and how to write work orders for lab techs. You'll learn how to measure faces for fitting, and how to adjust and repair frames. You'll be shown how to set up appointments, keep payrolls, and make sales.

 See what it's like to be an optician.

Depending on where you work, you'll have a chance to practice your skills in a formal apprenticeship at a large firm or in an informal learn-as-you-work program at a small business. Either way, you'll have a chance to gain hands-on-experience, working with customers as you adjust glasses, place orders, make sales, and place orders under the supervision of a seasoned pro.

Licensing requirements vary from state to state. Some states require you to complete apprenticeship programs and pass state or national certification exams. Even if it's not required in your state, earning certification from the American Board of Optometry, the National Contact Lens Examiners, or both shows potential employers that you've acquired the skills needed to work as an optician.

Learn the Lingo

Here are a few words to know as an optician:

- **Hypermetropia (farsightedness)** Difficulty focusing on close objects—for example, reading.

- **Myopia (nearsightedness)** The inability to see clearly at longer distances—for example when driving.

- **Presbyopia** A condition in which the eye's ability to focus diminishes as people grow older.

NOTES FROM THE FIELD

Optician, Greenfield, Massachusetts

Q: *How did you get your job?*

A: Actually, I was going to do something in optics and was transferring colleges when I got drafted and ended up going through the army's [optician] school. I had some family members involved in the business. I had a job waiting for me when I got out. My older cousin originally owned the business, and I went to work for him.

Q: *What do you like best about your job?*

A: Helping people see. There are some people who really need exotic eyewear to see properly. We know what's available and can sometimes help someone who has almost no vision see again. Some vision problems can only be cured through contact lenses, and that can be rewarding.

Q: *What's the most challenging part of your job?*

A: You're dealing with people—solving their eyewear problems.

Q: *What are the keys to success to being a dispensing optician?*

A: If you're going to work in retail, you need good people skills. You need a reasonably solid math background. A little bit of physics and geometry helps. You need good hand skills, as far as assembling the glasses.

Finding a Job

When you're ready to apply for a job, prepare a résumé showing off your skills, and make appointments with optical shops where you might want to work. Don't forget to line up references—former bosses and teachers who will put in a good word for you with prospective employers.

To give yourself an edge, make the effort to gain certification in your field. The American Board of Opticianry certifies those who dispense and work with spectacles while the National Contact Lens Examiners certifies those who work with contact lenses. Certification from one or both of these organizations shows prospective employers that you take your career seriously and have obtained the skills needed to do a good job.

Tips for Success

- Be a diplomat. For example, if a customer tries on a pair of unflattering glasses, you need to know how to steer him or her toward a more attractive pair without once rolling your eyes or scrunching your nose.

- Learn to run your own business. Many opticians are self-employed and hire help and manage the finances.

▲ An optician, after preparing a work order, collects payment from a customer.

Reality Check

Do you have a delicate touch and fine motor skills? After all, you must be careful when dealing with something as sensitive as the eye. And when you prepare lenses, you need to take extra care not to hurt yourself and others when you're cutting glass and working with machinery and chemicals.

Related Jobs to Consider

Licensed practical nurse (LPN). LPNs can administer most medications, change dressings, and perform other technical skills.

Phlebotomist. Phlebotomy technicians collect and label blood, urine, and other lab samples.

Pharmacy technician. Pharmacy technicians help pharmacists fill orders for prescriptions. Like optometrists, their jobs are part health care, part retail.

How to Move Up

- Become an optometrist. Optometrists are doctors who examine people's eyes to diagnose vision problems and eye diseases, in addition to fitting eyeglasses and contact lenses. You will have to complete a four-year program at an accredited optometry school. Another route is to become an ophthalmologist who handles surgery and diseases of the eye.

LEARN MORE ONLINE

AMERICAN BOARD OF OPTICIANRY/ NATIONAL CONTACT LENS EXAMINERS
The board and examiners certify opticians and ophthalmic dispensers who work with contact lenses. http://abo-ncle.org/

COMMISSION ON OPTICIANRY ACCREDITATION
This organization offers information on optician degree programs. http://www.coaccreditation.com

NATIONAL ACADEMY OF OPTICIANRY
This association is dedicated to the education and training of all opticians. http://www.nao.org

OPTICAL SOCIETY OF AMERICA.
This site discuss innovations related to sight. http://www.osa.org

OPTICIANS ASSOCIATION OF AMERICA
This organization exists to promote the optician profession. http://www.oaa.org

NATIONAL FEDERATION OF OPTICIANRY SCHOOLS
Find out more about training programs at this site. http://www.nfos.org

▲ An optician measures and prepares the lenses that will be fitted to the frames.

- Become a store manager. You can take on more of the business end by applying to be a store manager. As you gain more experience with a bigger firm, you may advance again to be a regional manager.

TEXT-DEPENDENT QUESTIONS

1. *What does a dispensing optician do?*

2. *What are some routes for getting trained in this field?*

3. *What is hypermetropia?*

4. *What are some related jobs you might consider?*

RESEARCH PROJECTS

1. *Start learning about eyes and how human vision works. You can ask your school librarian for reading recommendations, or start with "How Your Eyes Work" by the American Optometric Association (https://www.aoa.org/patients-and-public/resources-for-teachers/how-your-eyes-work).*

2. *If you are old enough, look for a part-time job at businesses that provide optical services. Whether you start off as a sales clerk or work in a formal apprenticeship program, you'll pick up important job skills and make key contacts in the industry.*

▲ As a dispensing optician, you may need to make small adjustments and minor repairs to customers' eyeglasses.

Medical Receptionist

Help doctors stay organized. Play a role in keeping people healthy. Deal with a variety of people.

4

WORDS TO UNDERSTAND

demeanor: outward attitude.

empathic: understanding the feelings of another person.

procedural: relating to the way things are usually done in a particular setting.

As the person who greets incoming patients, a medical receptionist sets the tone for the entire medical office. Consequently, first impressions are vital. You must be professional, courteous, respectful, and helpful. Because medical receptionists often deal with confidential information, you must also be discreet: you can't gossip about who doesn't have insurance coverage or chat about someone's medical condition.

When a patient arrives, you greet him or her, make note of his or her arrival, and verify information, such as the patient's current insurance provider, address, and phone number. You also answer the phones. Depending on the call, you may book an appointment, transfer the call to a nurse or doctor, or take a message.

Of the more than 1 million receptionists and information clerks employed in the United States, more than a third work in doctors' offices, hospitals, nursing homes, surgical centers, and other health care and social assistant outlets.

◀ A receptionist checks in patients at an orthopedist's office.

Is This Job Right for You?

To find out if being a medical receptionist is right for you, read each of the following questions and answer "Yes" or "No."

Yes	*No*	**1.**	*Do you have a friendly, caring manner?*
Yes	*No*	**2.**	*Do you work well with others?*
Yes	*No*	**3.**	*Are you discreet?*
Yes	*No*	**4.**	*Are you responsible and dependable?*
Yes	*No*	**5.**	*Do you take direction well?*
Yes	*No*	**6.**	*Are you sensitive to the needs of other people?*
Yes	*No*	**7.**	*Are you organized?*
Yes	*No*	**8.**	*Are you patient, and can you keep your emotions in check?*
Yes	*No*	**9.**	*Are you good with details?*
Yes	*No*	**10.**	*Do you have good judgment and know when to ask for help?*

If you answered "Yes" to most of these questions, consider a career as a medical receptionist. To find out more about this job, read on.

What's the Work Like?

As a medical receptionist, you are the first person most patients see when they enter a doctor's office or medical clinic. You greet the patient, make note of his or her arrival, review the patient's insurance coverage, and collect any payments. In between, you answer the phones, taking calls from patients who need your help scheduling an appointment, tracking down a medical record, or gaining a referral for a visit to a specialist. You may also perform other office tasks, such as faxing prescriptions to pharmacies, taking messages from other doctors, and calling patients to remind them about upcoming appointments.

TALKING MONEY

Salaries for medical receptionists and information clerks vary depending on where you work. The median hourly wage is $15.72 for those who work in dental offices, $14.14 for doctors' offices, and $13.20 for other health practitioners, according to 2016 data from the U.S. Bureau of Labor Statistics. The best-paid receptionists and information clerks earn more than $19.41 an hour.

▲ A medical receptionist may have to help patients fill out the required forms before they see the doctor.

To work as a medical receptionist, you need to be an efficient multitasker who can answer the phone, copy insurance cards, and input data into the computer, often all at the same time. Because you'll be dealing with lots of different people in a variety of situations, you also need excellent people skills. One moment, you may need to lend an **empathic** ear to a mother whose baby has a high fever. In the next moment, you may need to calm a patient who's upset by a long wait, or frustrated because his or her insurance is no longer valid. You also have some sense of who requires priority attention—if someone comes into the office and is gravely ill and needs immediate help, you rush them through to get medical care.

Who's Hiring?

- Doctors' offices

- Public, private, or federal hospitals, such as a veterans' hospital

- Medical clinics

- Personal care services

- Dental offices

Where Are the Jobs?

Making a first impression is important, so doctors' offices usually spend a little extra time and money creating an attractive reception area where the medical receptionists greet incoming patients. Depending on how big a practice is, you may work behind a single desk or in a work area shared by several receptionists. You may also work at a big hospital or clinic assisting a large volume of patients each day. Your work area is generally in plain view (and earshot) of waiting patients, so it's vital that you maintain a professional **demeanor** while you work and chat with coworkers.

▲ A receptionist reviews the day's schedule with the doctor.

Your hours will vary depending on where you work. If you work for a doctor who only sees patients Mondays through Fridays during the day, you'll probably work from 8 a.m. or 9 a.m. to 4 p.m. or 5 p.m. each day. If you work for a practice that also sees patients in the evenings or on the weekends, you may need to work during those times as well.

A Typical Day

Here are the highlights of a typical shift for a medical receptionist.

Greet incoming patients. Check the patient in and let the nurse know he or she has arrived. Verify that insurance, address, and other personal data are up to date. When a patient's name is called, direct the person to the appropriate waiting room.

Work the phones. Answer **procedural** questions, such as "How late is the office open on Saturday?" or "How do I obtain my child's medical records for summer camp?" Screen calls, taking messages as needed, and transferring urgent ones to the appropriate doctor or nurse. Help patients schedule future and urgent-care appointments to see the doctor.

Check out patients. After a patient sees the doctor, he or she may need your help scheduling a follow-up appointment, handling an insurance claim, or paying for the visit.

Perform office tasks. Open and sort mail, collect and distribute packages, collect and send faxes to pharmacies and other medical offices, and call patients to remind them about upcoming visits.

Start Preparing Now

- While in high school, enroll in classes that will help you develop computer, keyboarding, and other essential office skills. It pays to be a good typist.

- Taking courses in biology, health, and other medicine-related subject areas that can help you become familiar with scientific and medical terms.

TALKING TRENDS

Technology advances are transforming the role of medical receptionists. While they still answer the phones, a growing reliance on automated phone service has reduced the number of messages they need to take, freeing them up to take on more clerical responsibilities. Much of their work is done on a computer, where they type in a patient's insurance information, schedule appointments, and print medical records.

▲ A medical receptionist may have to collect co-payments, which vary by insurance plan. Collecting money is not always easy, but the best medical receptionists do it with a smile and grace.

- You may be able to pick up basic office skills by working as a secretary, treasurer, or a similar position in one of your school's clubs.

 Find out more about becoming a medical receptionist.

Training and How to Get It

To work as a medical receptionist, you generally need a high school diploma. Prospective employers prefer hiring candidates who are adept at working with computers and dealing with all kinds of people in a professional, courteous manner. Knowing basic office skills, such as how to operate a fax machine, distribute mail, answer the phones, and type will give you a competitive edge. You can often pick up these skills by volunteering at local nonprofit

NOTES FROM THE FIELD

Clerical coordinator, *Westchester County, New York*

Q: *How did you get your job?*

A: I started sending out résumés. I wasn't specifically looking for this. I got interviewed and liked what I saw. I started working as a front desk receptionist. Three years down the line, I joined the Westchester Medical Group and was offered a position as a clerical coordinator.

Q: *What do you like best about your job?*

A: Making patients happy. Patients usually have needs. They need questions answered. When I help a patient as much as I can, that makes my day.

　　Health care is an important profession. There is always going to be a job for whoever works in the field because everybody has to go to the doctor. That's why I'm staying here.

Q: *What's the most challenging part of your job?*

A: Coworkers. People have different personalities, so you have to deal with different personalities every day. It's hard when you expect someone to be like you and that person's not you.

Q: *What are the keys to success to being a medical receptionist?*

A: Basically, to succeed in this industry, you have to be patient and you have to be willing to do the work. That's what it comes down to—doing what you're supposed to do in a timely manner and being receptive to your coworkers' needs.

　　You have to be a people person. You have to have the ability to manage a lot of different entities—the doctors, the coworkers, the patients: It's a lot of different kinds of people you're going to be dealing with. So basically, that's the bottom line, you have to be a people person.

agencies, working part time for local businesses, or enrolling in an office skills course at a local community college or trade school. Because you're handling medical issues, some background in anatomy and physiology is practical.

Learn the Lingo

Here are a few terms related to the work of medical receptionists:

- **Proof of insurance** When a patient sees a doctor for the first time, the medical receptionist often asks to see the patient's "proof of insurance." Usually the patient produces a card issued by his or her insurance company. The card often includes the names of those covered under the policy, the dates of coverage, and contact information for the insurance company.

- **Preferred provider organization (PPO)** A medical receptionist can work for this type of health care organization, which provides health care services at a reduced fee.

- **Health maintenance organization (HMO)** Similar to a PPO, this is a group of doctors and other medical professionals offering care for a flat monthly rate.

Finding a Job

Send your résumé to office managers at local doctors' offices, medical clinics, and other medical facilities. Be sure to highlight relevant skills and experience and include references who can vouch for your dependability, character, and work ethic. Follow up with a phone call to see if you can schedule an interview. Even if the office doesn't have an opening, it can be helpful to meet workers in the field and see how they do their jobs.

You can also search your local newspaper or online job sites, many of which include listings for medical receptionists and information clerks.

Tips for Success

- Patience, patience. In your line of work, you'll have to deal with all sorts of personalities. The medical receptionist who can turn a disgruntled patient into a satisfied one will quickly become the office hero.

- Make reminder calls. Patients tend to forget appointments so be sure to call them the day before to make sure they're coming in for their scheduled visit.

▲ To be sure that the doctor's schedule is full but not overbooked, medical receptionists will need to confirm or reschedule appointments with patients.

Reality Check

Look in the mirror. Do you look polished? Because a medical receptionist is the first person patients see, it's important you show up for work looking like a professional with neatly combed hair, freshly clipped nails, and appropriate office wear—no scruffy jeans, wrinkled T-shirts, and the like.

Related Jobs to Consider

Medical transcriptionist. If you are an accurate typist and a good listener, you can work as a medical transcriptionist who transcribes, or types, recordings made by doctors—for medical reports, letters, and other health documents.

Medical assistant. The duties of a medical assistant vary from office to office. In addition to answering phones, greeting patients, and performing other clerical duties, medical assistants also often bring patients to the examining room, arrange the instruments and equipment in the rooms, and purchase and maintain the equipment and supplies.

How to Move Up

- Become a medical records technician. As a medical records technician, you're charged with keeping patients' medical records accurate and up-to-date, and filling requests to share the information with other doctors.

- Work as an office manager. In a busy medical clinic or group practice, you can work your way into a supervisory experience where you're responsible for scheduling and managing the work of other medical receptionists and information clerks.

LEARN MORE ONLINE

NATIONAL ASSOCIATION OF PROFESSIONAL RECEPTIONISTS
This group promotes professionalism, pride, and expertise for receptionists. http://www.receptionists.us

AMERICAN HEALTH INFORMATION MANAGEMENT ASSOCIATION
This organization is dedicated to educating and advancing those in health information management. http://www.ahima.org

AMERICAN ASSOCIATION OF MEDICAL ASSISTANTS
All medical assistants find practical information at this site. http://www.aama-ntl.org

NATIONAL SOCIETY OF ALLIED HEALTH
This association is committed to improving the health care status of African Americans and "at-risk" populations, including economically disadvantaged populations, through education, employment, community service, and research. http://www.nsah.org

TEXT-DEPENDENT QUESTIONS

1. *What do medical receptionists do?*

2. *What are important qualities for a medical receptionist to have?*

3. *How does someone get trained for this job?*

4. *How might someone move up in this job?*

RESEARCH PROJECTS

1. *If you are of age, volunteer as a receptionist at a nonprofit organization or work part time at a local business. This experience can give you experience that will come in handy when you start looking for work as a medical receptionist.*

2. *Helping patients navigate their health insurance and dealing with insurance paperwork are often the most challenging parts of working in a medical office. Start familiarizing yourself with the fast-changing world of health insurance by exploring the site hosted by Medical Billing and Coding Certification (http://www.medicalbillingandcoding.org/health-insurance-guide/overview).*

▲ Although there has been a big push for making all medical records electronic, physical files are still widely used.

Veterinary Assistant/ Laboratory Animal Caretaker

5

Save animal lives. Comfort pet owners.
Learn medical skills.

WORDS TO UNDERSTAND

accredited: describes something that's been officially recognized, such as an educational program.

clerical: refers to routine office tasks, such as typing, filing, or filling out paperwork.

euthanize: to put a living being to death in a humane way.

For animal lovers, a career as a veterinary assistant can be an ideal job. In this career, you get to help the veterinarian care for animals. When an owner brings a pet in for treatment, you gather information about the animal's medical history and enter the data into the computer. You then bring the animal into the treatment area. Depending on what the veterinarian requests, you may need to restrain a dog while the vet gives it a shot, take an X-ray of a cat's leg, or trim a guinea pig's nails. You also often bathe, feed, and groom the animals, and you might also assist during surgeries, preparing equipment beforehand and helping out during the procedure. Laboratory animal caretakers perform similar tasks, but in a lab setting rather than a vet's office.

◀ A veterinary assistant welcomes a pet owner and his dog for an annual checkup.

▲ A laboratory animal caretaker examines a mouse used in research.

Besides caring for animals, veterinary assistants also help the pets' owners. For example, as a vet assistant you might show an owner how to change a pet's bandage or offer condolences when a pet dies.

Is This Job Right for You?

To find out if being a veterinary assistant is a good fit for you, read each of the following questions and answer "Yes" or "No."

Yes	*No*	**1.**	*Do you work well with animals?*
Yes	*No*	**2.**	*Are you pleasant when dealing with other people?*
Yes	*No*	**3.**	*Are you good with details?*
Yes	*No*	**4.**	*Are you reliable?*
Yes	*No*	**5.**	*Are you organized?*
Yes	*No*	**6.**	*Do you follow directions well?*
Yes	*No*	**7.**	*Can you write detailed, accurate reports?*
Yes	*No*	**8.**	*Can you handle* **clerical** *duties, such as answering the phones, scheduling appointments, and taking payments?*
Yes	*No*	**9.**	*Can you be empathetic with pet owners who are worried about their animals?*
Yes	*No*	**10.**	*Are you comfortable cleaning up after animals?*

If you answered "Yes" to most of these questions, consider a career as a veterinary assistant. To find out more about this job, read on.

What's the Work Like?

As an assistant, you help veterinarians and veterinary technicians care for animals in vet offices, clinics, shelters, zoos, laboratories, and other locales. In veterinary offices, you greet customers and their pets, schedule appointments, handle payments, and answer the phones. If you work the front desk, you're the first person the pet owner sees, so it's important to present yourself as a well-groomed professional who cares about the customer and his or her pet.

You also will have a chance to help the veterinarian and veterinary technician examine and treat

> **TALKING MONEY**
>
> The average annual salary of veterinary assistants and laboratory animal caretakers was $25,250 according to 2016 data from the U.S. Bureau of Labor Statistics. Top earners in the field made more than $37,8100 a year. Median hourly earnings were about $12.14.

▲ A veterinary assistant holds a cat while the veterinarian reviews the X-rays.

pets. Depending on the animal's needs, you may need to restrain a pet while the veterinarian examines it or gives it a vaccination. You may be asked to take X-rays or draw blood from an animal. You will also bathe animals, feed and water them, and brush and cut their hair.

Some veterinary assistants work for vets who specialize in treating large animals, such as cows and horses. In that role, you may be asked to go to the ranch to help care for an injured horse or to vaccinate cows. Keeping accurate records is an important part of your job. When an animal receives a rabies shot, a

TALKING TRENDS

Pet owners who are willing to pay for advanced care are creating a growing need for advanced veterinary care, increasing the job opportunities for skilled veterinary assistants. Meanwhile, demand for lab animals is also expected to grow, as the biomedical research field expands and other organizations work to address food safety issues and other public health problems. Employment of veterinary assistants and laboratory animal caretakers is expected to grow faster than average for all occupations through the year 2024, according to the Bureau of Labor Statistics.

vaccine, or another treatment, you'll be responsible for recording the data in the computer or on the animal's paper chart.

Just like in a hospital or doctor's office, emergencies can play havoc with even the best-planned schedule. When an animal comes in requiring immediate attention, you'll have to juggle the schedule to find time to handle the emergency. At such times, you may end up working late and may not even have a chance to eat lunch.

One of the toughest parts of your job will be dealing with animals that are seriously ill or injured. In fact, there will be times when you will have to help the veterinarian **euthanize** an animal. Putting a gravely ill animal "to sleep" can be especially tough for veterinary workers because people who go into this field generally do so because they love animals.

Who's Hiring?

- Veterinary offices

- Animal hospitals

- Veterinary clinics

- Pet stores

- Animal shelters

- Kennels

- Humane Society

Where Are the Jobs?

Veterinary assistants work wherever vets work. They work in private veterinary practices, animal clinics, and animal hospitals. Some also work inside pet stores, diagnostic labs, and in animal shelters. Veterinary assistants who care for small animals, such as cats, dogs, and birds, generally work indoors, while those who care for larger animals, such as horses and cows, often drive to farms and ranches to care for animals.

Watch a day in the life of a veterinary assistant.

A Typical Day

Here are the highlights of a typical shift for a veterinary assistant.

Get ready, set, and go. Make sure examining rooms are fully stocked with needed supplies. Return messages left by pet owners from the previous evening. Help the vet technicians prepare the day's charts for the incoming patients.

Take care of patients and their owners. When owners bring their animals in to see the vet, you greet the clients, sign them in, and handle any necessary paper work. Provide emotional support to owners whose pets are ill.

▲ A veterinary assistant must be good at multitasking. This veterinary assistant organizes files for the day while scheduling appointments on the phone.

Keep the office running. Handle pet owners as they call in, record visits in the calendar, process payments, and make reminder calls for future appointments. Keep an eye on the supplies, and reorder as needed.

Care for the animals. You may, for example, hold a dog while the vet technician gives it a shot. Depending on the pet's needs, you may clip its nails, trim its hair, or brush its teeth. If the animal is staying overnight for observation, you may need to feed, bathe, groom and walk the animal, and also keep its sleeping area clean.

Start Preparing Now

- While in high school, take courses in science, health, communications, and office skills.

- At some schools, you may be able to enroll in a vocational tech program that focuses on veterinary assistant skills.

- You can also gain experience in a part-time or summer job at an animal clinic, nature center, or pet shop.

Training and How to Get It

Most veterinary assistants and laboratory animal caretakers receive their training on the job. You can also pick up skills by enrolling in an assistant veterinary training course offered via vocational programs in high schools, community colleges, trade schools, and online distance-learning programs. Before you sign up, though, make sure the program is **accredited** by a professional veterinary association, such as the National Association of Veterinary Technicians in America. During your training, you'll learn how to schedule appointments, deal with grieving clients, handle medical records, bathe and groom pets, and perform other vital skills.

Learn the Lingo

Here are a few words to know as a veterinary assistant:

- **Rabies** A deadly viral infection that is transmitted from animal bites. As a veterinary assistant, you will help prepare and document mandatory vaccinations for rabies and other diseases.

- **Round worms** A common internal parasite for dogs.

Finding a Job

Reach out to the managers at local animal hospitals, veterinary offices, pet stores, kennels, and animal clinics. Be sure to bring a résumé that highlights your strengths and skills, and include references who can vouch for your dependability, work ethic, and ability to work with animals.

If there isn't an immediate opening for a veterinary assistant position, consider accepting another entry-level job in animal care. You could, for example, gain experience working as a pet groomer at a grooming salon, as a sales clerk in a pet store, or as a bather or brusher in a kennel. You also may be able to get job leads from professional associations, such as the National Association of Veterinary Technicians in America and the American Veterinary Medical Association.

LEARN MORE ONLINE

AMERICAN ASSOCIATION FOR LABORATORY ANIMAL SCIENCE
This site specializes in educational materials for those pursuing a career in lab animal science. http://www.aalas.org

AMERICAN ANIMAL HOSPITAL ASSOCIATION
Education, programs, and services to help veterinary practices are provided here. http://www.aahanet.org

AMERICAN VETERINARY MEDICAL ASSOCIATION
This organization provides everything you need to know about veterinary medicine. http://www.avma.org

NATIONAL ASSOCIATION OF VETERINARY TECHNICIANS IN AMERICA
Future veterinary technicians find resources here. http://www.navta.net

VET MED TEAM
This group provides educational resources for those involved with veterinary medicine. http://www.vetmedteam.com

Tips for Success

- Like people as much as pets. If you want to be a veterinary assistant, chances are you work well with animals. But to be successful in this job, you also must be good at dealing with the animals' owners, who may at times be angry, frustrated, or even distraught over a pet's death.

- Hone your communication skills. You have to be a good listener when pet owners describe ailments, and you have to relay that information accurately to the veterinarian.

NOTES FROM THE FIELD

Veterinary assistant, Gunnison, Colorado

Q: *How did you get your job?*

A: I wanted a job while I was going to college. I started working in retail and I decided I didn't like that. I wanted something that was important to me. I decided to apply at Town and Country Animal Hospital because I love animals.

Q: *What is the most challenging part of the job?*

A: Sometimes we have long days. Like for instance, yesterday, we had such a long day, I think a lot of us ended up working 13 hours without any break. We had an emergency come in so we had to skip lunch. We had a cow come in that we had to do an emergency C-section on.

Q: *What do you like best about your job?*

A: I think the best part of the job is when an animal comes in ill and then watching it get better and knowing you had a part in that. You get to do a lot of stuff—you get to draw blood, take X-rays. It's a lot like being a veterinarian, so if you're thinking of going into veterinary medicine, working as a veterinary assistant will give you an idea of what it will be like. I love what I do and am thinking about becoming a certified veterinary tech.

Q: *What are the keys to success to being a veterinary assistant?*

A: You have to be a hard worker. You need to care about animals. I care about animals. I don't want to see them hurt or suffer, and that motivates me to do a good job and do whatever I can to help them. Compassion is also a big one. You have to be tough emotionally, because there are statistics out there that veterinarians and people who work at veterinary clinics see deaths more than people doctors do, because animals have a shorter life span.

Reality Check

Animals die. And sometimes when they're really sick, you may be asked to help "put them to sleep." For animal lovers, this can be a gut-wrenching experience, and you need to make sure you're emotionally able to handle it.

Related Jobs to Consider

Dental assistant. Like veterinary assistants, dental assistants help keep dental offices running. They schedule appointments, greet patients, handle insurance, and often help the dentist while he or she is treating patients.

Medical receptionist. Medical receptionists help keep doctors' offices and hospitals running smoothly. They schedule appointments, answer phones, make follow-up phone calls, and handle a variety of paperwork.

How to Move Up

- Become a vet technician. To become a veterinary technician, you need to complete an associate's degree at an accredited school. With the additional training comes more responsibility for pet care, and of course, more money.

- Look into a career as a vet technologist. If you later decide to go for a four-year degree, you can become a veterinary technologist. As a veterinary technologist, you get to perform more complex procedures and often can move into supervisory roles.

TEXT-DEPENDENT QUESTIONS

1. *If you enjoy working outdoors, what kind of animals would you want to work with?*

2. *What is required to become a veterinary technician?*

3. *What is the most emotionally stressful part of the job?*

▲ Some veterinary assistants take care of large animals, such as cows or horses.

RESEARCH PROJECTS

1. *Get started learning about animal care taking by volunteering at a local animal shelter, or become active in a Future Farmers of America or 4-H program in your area.*

2. *Learn about the veterinary field by checking out these books:* Veterinary Medicine: An Illustrated History *by Robert H. Dunlop and* Shelter Medicine for Veterinarians and Staff *by Lila Miller. Also look for the works of James Herriot, a famous British veterinarian and author.*

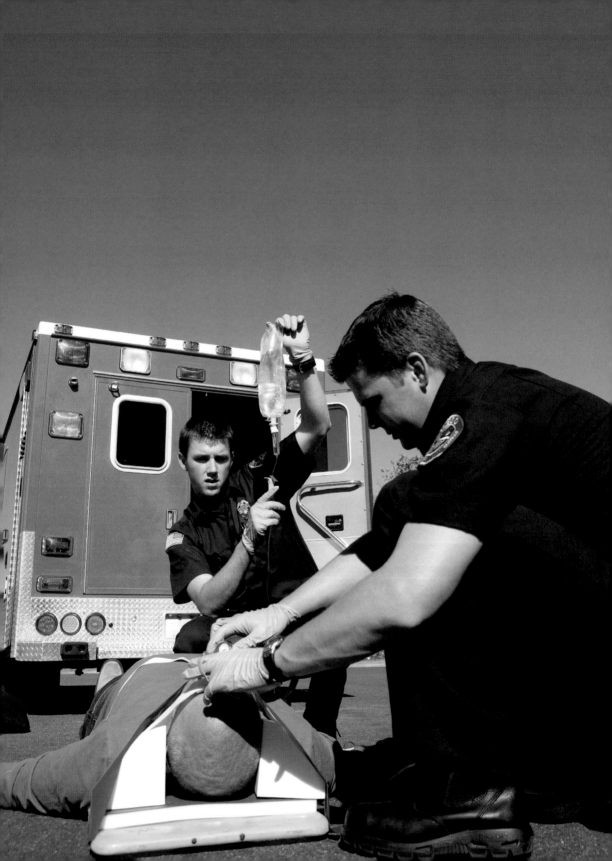

Emergency Medical Technician/Paramedic

6

Save lives. Rush to the rescue at the scene of a crime or accident. Learn medical skills.

WORDS TO UNDERSTAND

cardiac: having to do with the heart.

electrocardiogram: a test that monitors the electrical activity of the heart.

respiratory: having to do with breathing.

stabilized: here, when a patient's condition is unlikely to suddenly get worse.

If you work well under pressure, you might have what it takes to work as an emergency medical technician (EMT) or paramedic. When a child is discovered face down in a pool, a construction worker falls from a roof, or a diabetic has an insulin reaction at work, an EMT often arrives at the scene first. As an EMT or paramedic, you're trained to recognize and treat life-threatening emergencies outside a hospital. You provide initial care to patients with conditions such as a stroke, a seizure, or a severe asthma attack. You also rush medical assistance to people who suffer traumatic injuries, such as broken bones, severe burns, and stab wounds. Once a patient is **stabilized**, you transport the injured or ill person to an emergency room (ER) where trained doctors and nurses can give more advanced medical help.

◀ A team of paramedics administers an IV to stabilize a man who has been in a car collision.

While money is, of course, important, for EMT workers, the job itself is the real reward. Whether it's holding a scared child's hand while he's being transported to a hospital or reviving a heart-attack victim with a lifesaving treatment, EMT workers know they make a difference in people's lives.

Is This Job Right for You?

To find out if being an EMT or paramedic is a good fit for you, read each of the following questions and answer "Yes" or "No."

Yes	*No*	1. *Do you like helping others?*
Yes	*No*	2. *Are you physically fit and strong enough to help move or lift patients into an ambulance?*
Yes	*No*	3. *Do you have good driving skills?*
Yes	*No*	4. *Do you work well under stress and have what it takes to handle the pressure of dealing with life-and-death situations?*
Yes	*No*	5. *Do you have good coordination? Can you stay balanced while working in awkward positions and do you have the fine motor skills needed to perform intricate maneuvers on patients?*
Yes	*No*	6. *Do you have solid math skills and the ability to quickly and accurately make calculations in your head?*
Yes	*No*	7. *Do you have good eyesight?*
Yes	*No*	8. *Are you emotionally stable?*
Yes	*No*	9. *Are you a fast, accurate worker?*
Yes	*No*	10. *Do you have a strong stomach—can you can handle the sight of blood and broken bones?*

If you answered "Yes" to most of these questions, consider a career as an EMT. To find out more about this job, read on.

What's the Work Like?

Because an emergency can happen anytime of the day, EMTs don't work a typical 9-to-5 shift. As an EMT or paramedic, your workweek can run from 45 to 60 hours, and you may be on the job at any time of the day or night.

On the job, you provide initial care to patients with conditions such as cardiac arrest, a reaction to poison, or a severe asthma attack. You also care for people who suffer traumatic injuries, such as gunshot wounds, severe burns, and concussions from a fall.

Depending on the problem, an EMT may need to bandage and splint a broken arm, administer nitroglycerin to a heart patient, or immobilize a patient on a backboard before putting him or her on a stretcher. All this will be done under the supervision of a doctor, who communicates with the emergency workers via radio transmissions.

TALKING MONEY

The annual median salary for EMTs and paramedics is $32,670 a year with the top 10 percent making more than $56,310 a year, according to 2016 data from the U.S. Bureau of Labor Statistics. EMT workers who are employed as part of a fire or police department may be covered by pension plans that provide half pay after 20 to 25 years. EMT workers often supplement their pay by teaching cardiopulmonary resuscitation (CPR) courses and EMT classes at community colleges.

The job of paramedic is very similar to EMTs, except that paramedics have even more training. One of the big differences between being a basic EMT and a paramedic is that paramedics can give shots, start intravenous lifelines, and use more advanced airway management devices to support breathing. Paramedics can also use **electrocardiogram** (EKG) machines and other high-tech equipment.

On the way to the hospital, one EMT drives while the other cares for the patient and monitors the patient's vital signs. Two EMTs typically command an ambulance or "rig," so you'll get to know your partner well with all the time you spend hurrying to answer distress calls and speeding patients to the hospital. When the ambulance arrives at the hospital, you turn the patient over to the medical staff, letting the doctors and nurses know how the patient is doing and what treatment has been provided. You then ready the van for the next patient, and when another call comes in, you speed off to help yet another patient.

Who's Hiring?

• City and county governments

• Local fire departments

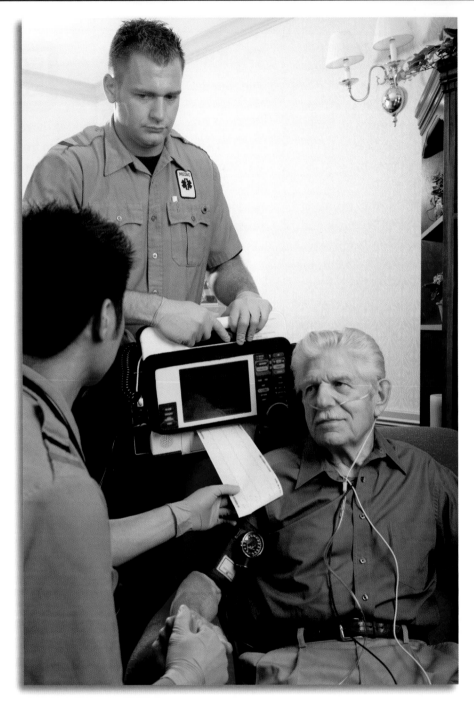

▲ Paramedics use an electrocardiogram machine to check a patient's heart activity after he collapsed in his home.

- Hospitals
- Privately run companies that provide emergency care

Where Are the Jobs?

Emergency workers are always on the go. You'll put in a lot of hours racing around in your rig, rushing to reach people who need emergency care and then staying with them while they're transported to a medical facility. You go wherever the emergency is—be it on the side of a highway, on a playground,

or inside someone's home. Your job environment will depend on where you work. If you work in a big city, you're going to be on the run nearly all the time. On a busy day, you could answer as many as 15 to 30 calls in one 24-hour period. If you work near the interstate, you'll probably deal with a lot of motor vehicle accidents. If you're near an inner city, you'll probably handle more gunshot wounds, stabbings, and drug-related overdoses. If you work in a rural area, the pace will be somewhat slower, and you'll often have to drive farther to reach people who need emergency care.

A Typical Day

Here are the highlights of a typical shift for an EMT worker.

Check your vehicle. When you arrive at your station, check the gas and oil in your rig. You don't want to be held back by an empty tank. Kick the tires to make sure they're full of air.

Review your supplies. You also need to go over the medical supplies in your vehicle to make sure you have enough equipment to treat patients during your shift.

Wait for a 911 dispatcher to send you to a scene. When you finally get a call, you and your EMT partner go to the scene as quickly and safely as you can.

NOTES FROM THE FIELD

Nationally registered EMT, Marion, Illinois

Q: *How did you get your job?*

A: I started as a military medic. Part of my rotation was through a military hospital. I spent time working where the medical technicians worked. I spent two weeks in an emergency room. It just sort of triggered something. The air force didn't require basic EMT training back then so I took a basic EMT program on my own at a local community college.

Q: *What do you like best about your job?*

A: What it really comes down to is helping people. At the end of the day, that patient who you knew was on the borderline of going either way, it's knowing that what you did made a difference. A lot of EMTs will go back and ask, "What happened to Mr. Smith? He was in full cardiac arrest when we brought him here. Where is he and how is he doing?" The bottom line is, it's a great career for people who have that mindset of "I really want to make a difference; I want to help people."

Q: *What's the most challenging part of your job?*

A: The motivation for people who typically get into emergency medical service is very altruistic. They want to help people. They want to save lives. Unfortunately, that's one of the bubbles we burst in class: you're not going to save everybody.

Q: *What are the keys to success to being an EMT?*

A: In a perfect world, we would like to see somebody with fairly solid math skills. When you do drug calculations, you're working with fractions and decimals. We'd like to see people better prepared in their writing ability. After every run, you have to fill out a report.

Assess the situation at the scene. You make sure you and your vehicle are not in danger before you enter the scene. You assess the patient's condition if it's just one person. You do triage if it's a multiple accident. Triage is a system for prioritizing who gets attention first, taking care of the most seriously injured first. You try to stabilize them and put them in the back of the rig.

Rush to the medical facility. You (or your partner) drive the ambulance while the other EMT worker looks after the patient. If driving, you have to be fast but careful, and warn other drivers you're coming through by turning on your rooftop emergency lights. Once you arrive at the ER, you provide the ER workers with vital information about the patient's status and any treatment administered on the way.

Wait for the next call. After you've successfully delivered the patient to the ER doctors and nurses, you and your EMT teammate catch your breath until you receive another call from the dispatcher.

▲ An EMT informs the 911 dispatcher that she and her partner are en route to the next emergency call.

Start Preparing Now

- You can get a jump on your career while still in high school by doing well in math and writing courses. As an EMT, you may need to quickly calculate how much of a drug to administer to a patient. Depending on how advanced you are in your career, you may have to give a syringe with a few mL (milliliters) of a medicine, for example. You'll also need to write accurate medical reports on the patients you treat.

- Volunteer or intern at a local hospital or medical facility. This experience can help you gain a better understanding of the health field. And it could eventually lead to a permanent job.

- Once you start your training, sign up for as many training hours as you can. An entry level, or first responder, needs about 40 hours of training. Once you complete that, you can train to become an EMT-Basic, or EMT-1. Eventually, you can work your way up to an EMT-Paramedic, which requires about 1,000 hours of training, and commands the highest wages. Paramedic programs often award two-year degrees.

- While in school, take time to reach out to professional organizations in your field. You can, for example, become a student member of the National Association of Emergency Medical Technicians (NAEMT). Doing so will give you a chance to meet others in the field and can often provide leads to future jobs.

Training and How to Get It

A high school diploma is all you need to get started in a formal EMT training program. You can investigate EMT and paramedic programs at community colleges, technical schools, hospitals, EMS academies, and universities. Different states have varying requirements, so you should check with your state's emergency medical services office, which is listed on the National Registry of Emergency Medical Technicians' site (http://www.nremt.org). You can also check with the Committee on Accreditation of Educational Programs for the Emergency Medical Services Professions (http://www.coaemsp.org). The National Highway Traffic Safety Administration (NHTSA) sets the training requirements for different EMT levels while individual states oversee the actual certification process. Most states require EMTs and paramedics to be certified by the National Registry of Emergency Medical Technicians.

Your EMT training will occur in stages. During your basic training, you'll be taught how to assess a patient's condition and deal with **respiratory**, trauma, and **cardiac** emergencies.

You'll learn how to handle bleeding, broken bones, blocked airways, and emergency child-birth. While you're mastering emergency skills, you'll have a chance to work with a variety of splints, bandages, suction devices, oxygen, stretchers, backboards, and other emergency equipment. After you finish the required training and pass a written and practical exam, you'll be eligible to work as an EMT-Basic. You'll also be eligible to pursue additional training to qualify as an EMT-Intermediate. During this next stage, you'll learn how to give patients fluids intravenously, operate advanced airway devices, and perform other advanced procedures. The most advanced level—that of a paramedic—requires even more training (more than 1,000 hours), additional clinical experience, and the successful completion of a written and practical exam.

Because medical care is constantly changing, emergency medical workers are always learning new techniques. In fact, to stay certified, most states require EMTs and paramedics to meet various continuing education requirements.

Learn the Lingo

Here are a few words to know as an EMT:

- **Vital signs** These are the signs of life. They include a person's body temperature, pulse rate, respiration rate, and blood pressure.

- **CPR** Short for *cardiopulmonary resuscitation*, CPR is an emergency first aid procedure given to victims of cardiac arrest, involving blowing into the patient's mouth and pumping the person's chest.

- **Defibrillator** An emergency device designed to shock the heart with an electrical current to restore a normal pulse. (You may have seen a defibrillator used on a TV medical drama—an EMT applies two pads or paddles to the patient, and sometimes yells "Clear!" meaning to stand clear.)

Finding a Job

Check to see who provides emergency care in your area. Depending on where you live, EMTs may work directly for

See what it's like to be an EMT.

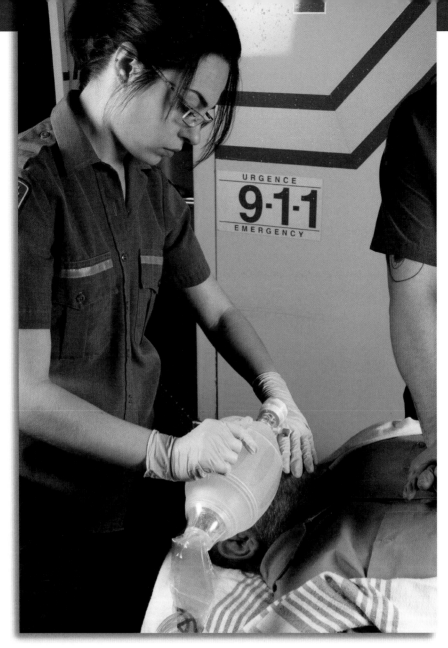

▲ EMTs administer CPR to an unconscious patient with the assistance of an air bag.

hospitals, for local governments, or for private companies. Your EMT instructor most likely can help you sort out who does what and may even be able to put you in touch with a hiring supervisor. Be sure to bring proof of your training and certification and present yourself as a responsible, dependable worker.

Tips for Success

- Keep your emotions in check. When you respond to an emergency, you have to stay focused on providing the care the patient needs. You can't let yourself be rattled by the chaos or hysteria of worried family members.

- Relieve stress. This is a very stressful and emotional job, and you'll need an outlet to relax and recharge so you don't burn out. Make time to play a sport, go to the movies, and do the things that you enjoy.

Reality Check

It's great when you save someone's life. But can you handle the letdown that occurs when someone dies before you can get the person to the ER? To have a long-lasting career in emergency work, you have to be able to handle the emotional highs and lows of working in lifesaving situations.

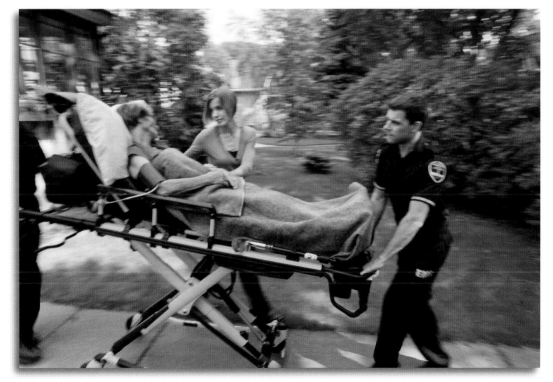

▲ EMTs rush out of a house to get a patient to the hospital as soon as possible.

Related Jobs to Consider

Phlebotomist. Phlebotomy technicians collect and label blood, urine, and other lab samples.

Licensed practical nurse (LPN). LPNs can administer most medications, change dressings, and perform other technical skills.

How to Move Up

- Become a paramedic. EMTs who complete about 1,000 hours of training can become a paramedic. Paramedics are qualified to perform more complicated procedures and command the highest wages. Experienced paramedics with leadership skills can often work as supervisors. They can, for example, work as an operation manager or an administrative director of emergency services.

- Earn a degree as a registered nurse (RN). To become an RN, you'll need a two-year associate's degree or a four-year bachelor's degree. Registered nurses, especially those with four-year degrees, can often move into supervisory positions.

- Look into advanced training to be a physical therapy technician, a surgical technician, or a laboratory technician.

TEXT-DEPENDENT QUESTIONS

1. *What types of health issues does an EMT deal with?*

2. *What's the difference between an EMT and a paramedic?*

3. *What is a defibrillator for?*

4. *How might you move up in this field?*

RESEARCH PROJECTS

1. *Check out one or more of these excellent memoirs, which will make you feel like you are riding along in the back of the ambulance:* Lights and Sirens *by Kevin Grange;* Paramedic *by Peter Canning; or* A Thousand Naked Strangers *by Kevin Hazzard.*

2. *Start learning about how to help people in health emergencies by taking a course in CPR or other first aid techniques. You can search online by typing "first aid class" and your area, or you can search the database of the American Heart Association (http://cpr.heart.org/AHAECC/CPRAndECC/FindACourse/UCM_473162_Find-A-Course.jsp).*

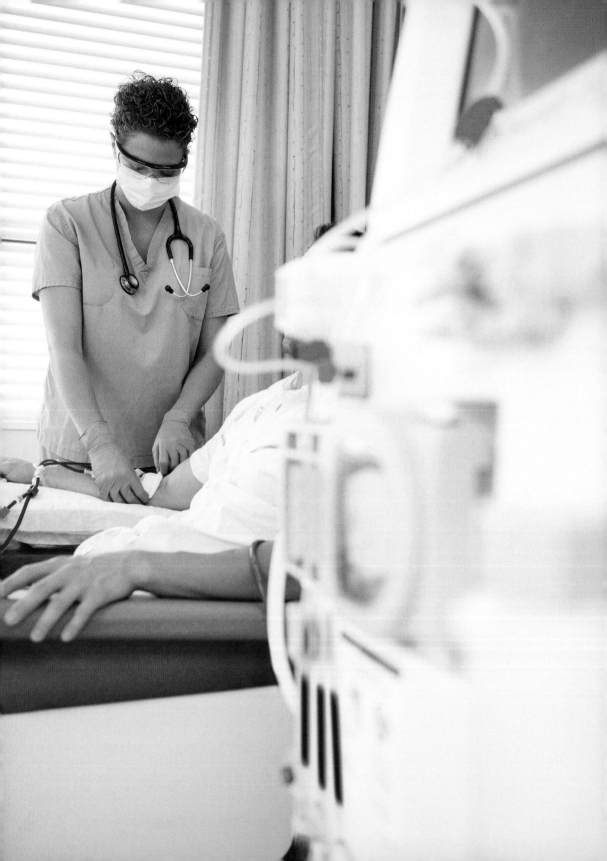

Dialysis Technician

Comfort patients. Operate sophisticated equipment. Save lives.

7

WORDS TO UNDERSTAND

cardiopulmonary resuscitation: a life-saving technique for people who have stopped breathing or whose hearts have stopped.

empathic: understanding the feelings of another person.

nephrologist: kidney doctor.

sterilize: to make something completely free of all microorganisms.

I f you like helping people and are good with technology, you might enjoy a career as a dialysis technician. Dialysis technicians play a vital role in keeping people alive: they operate dialysis machines that filter extra water, minerals, and toxins from the blood of patients whose kidneys can no longer do so. Without these lifesaving treatments, patients with poorly functioning kidneys would die. Dialysis is a life-support treatment, not a cure for kidney disease.

A dialysis technician prepares the equipment for a patient, monitors it while it's being used, and cleans and sterilizes it afterward. Working under the supervision of **nephrologists** and registered nurses, dialysis technicians also keep tabs on patients during the treatment.

◀ A technician administers renal dialysis treatment to a patient.

They measure and adjust the flow of blood, and measure and adjust the rate of the fluid that's being removed. During treatment, they keep a close eye on patients' vital signs, checking and recording weight and temperature. If something goes wrong, dialysis technicians have to respond quickly. Depending on the problem, the technician may need to page the doctor for assistance or start giving a patient **cardiopulmonary resuscitation (CPR)**.

Because many dialysis patients receive treatment on an ongoing basis, they often come to view their dialysis technicians as confidants with whom they can share their concerns, so being a good listener is a big plus in this field.

Is This Job Right for You?

To find out if being a dialysis technician is a good fit for you, read each of the following questions and answer "Yes" or "No."

Yes	*No*	1. *Can you work with people who are very ill?*
Yes	*No*	2. *Do you have a friendly, caring manner?*
Yes	*No*	3. *Do you have good stamina and can you be on your feet for hours?*
Yes	*No*	4. *Are you strong enough to lift heavy objects?*
Yes	*No*	5. *Are you careful with detail and do you avoid cutting corners?*
Yes	*No*	6. *Are you sensitive to the needs of other people?*
Yes	*No*	7. *Can you follow specific rules and regulations?*
Yes	*No*	8. *Can you handle stress?*
Yes	*No*	9. *Can you accurately monitor gauges, dials, and other indicators?*
Yes	*No*	10. *Are you a good listener?*

If you answered "Yes" to most of these questions, consider a career as a dialysis technician. To find out more about this job, read on.

Who's Hiring?

• Hospitals and medical clinics that provide dialysis treatments

• Clinics that specialize in dialysis treatments

• Home-care services that offer dialysis treatments in patients' homes

What's the Work Like?

As a dialysis technician, you'll run the machines that remove the waste and excess fluids from the blood of patients whose kidneys can no longer function properly. A big part of your job is to make sure the equipment is ready for each patient: you clean, **sterilize**, and inspect the equipment before and after each use. You also help set up the machine and connect it to the patients.

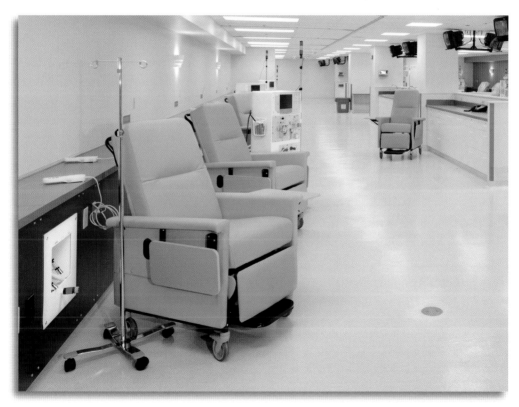

▲ When working at a dialysis clinic or treatment center, such as the one pictured here, it is important to clean and inspect the equipment before each use. All equipment must be sterilized before a patient comes in for treatment.

During dialysis, you monitor a patient's vital signs and blood flow, making sure everything is going smoothly. Once the patient's dialysis treatment is complete, you disconnect the patient from the machine, discard the used supplies, and sanitize the equipment so it'll be ready for the next patient.

Because patients receive treatments on an ongoing basis, many feel comfortable talking to their dialysis technicians about their nutritional, physical, and emotional concerns. As you lend an **empathetic** ear, be sure to make note of any information that the patient's doctor might need to know. The information you share can often help the doctor take better care of the patient.

 Find out more about becoming a dialysis technician.

Where Are the Jobs?

Your job environment will vary depending on what type of employer you choose. If you work in a hospital, you'll work in a building that provides a variety of care, including dialysis treatments, to its patients. If you work in a facility or for a doctor who specializes in dialysis treatment, you'll work in a setting where all the resources—both the workers and the machinery—are devoted to caring for patients with kidney problems.

Some dialysis technicians provide dialysis treatment in their patients' homes. If you provide home care, part of your day will be spent driving from one patient's home to the next. Your hours will be determined by your employer's and the patients' needs. Some clinics open early in the morning, stay open at night, and offer treatment during the weekends. Dialysis technicians who work weekends and nights are often rewarded with a higher wage, so it often pays to be flexible with your schedule.

TALKING TRENDS

The job outlook for dialysis technicians looks bright. As the population grows older and people live longer, more people are apt to develop kidney problems that will require dialysis treatment. Employment for all medical assistants is expected to grow by about 23 percent—much faster than average for all occupations—through the year 2024, according to the Bureau of Labor Statistics.

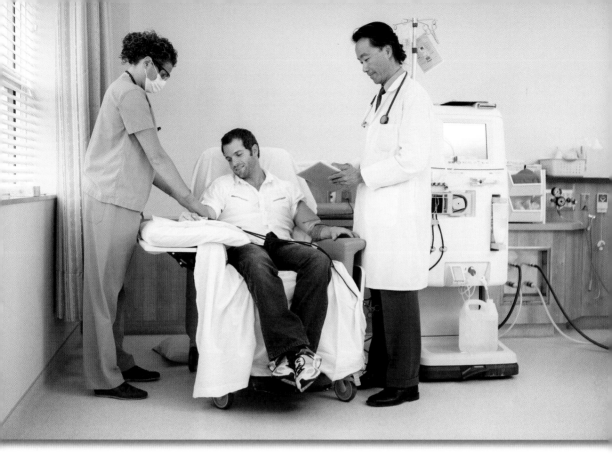

▲ A dialysis technician, working in a hospital, talks her patient through the treatment with the doctor present.

A Typical Day

Here are the highlights of a typical shift as a dialysis technician.

Check the equipment. You want to make sure your machinery is clean and in working order. You'll test the alarms, the conductivity, and the temperature settings on the monitors and devices.

Review patient's health status. When a patient arrives, you'll check predialysis vital signs, weight, and temperature. You'll administer local anesthesia, insert the needles, and start the patient's dialysis treatment.

Monitor treatment. During the treatment, you'll measure and adjust the blood flow rates, calculate and adjust the fluid removal rates, and pay close attention to the patient's vital signs.

Stay watchful. You'll keep an eye out for emergencies, such as a blood leak or a blood clot.

Record posttreatment measurements/observations. When the patient's dialysis treatment is done, you'll check the patient's vital signs, temperature, and weight, and let the supervising nurse know about any emotional, nutritional, or medical concerns that the patient may have mentioned during the treatment.

Clean up. You'll return the equipment to the reuse room, where you'll clean and sterilize it so it's ready for the next patient.

Start Preparing Now

- Look for a vocational-education course or program in health careers at your high school.

- Take science classes in subjects like biology that help you understand how the body works.

- Volunteer or seek part-time work at health care clinics, nursing homes, and other medical facilities to see if the health care field is right for you. That way you can get a real sense of what it's like to work with patients.

Training and How to Get It

High school graduates can enroll in dialysis technician training programs at community colleges and technical institutes throughout the country. Many employers also provide on-the-job training to promising job candidates. Programs usually last 6 to 12 weeks and include a mix of classroom and hands-on clinical work. During training, you'll learn why kidneys are so important and how dialysis helps patients with kidney problems. You'll also learn how to operate the dialysis equipment and what to look for before, during, and after treatment. When you finish your training, you'll be awarded a certificate or technical diploma that lets prospective employers know you've completed the training needed to become a dialysis technician.

To become certified, you must take approved medical courses and pass exams given by the Board of Nephrology Examiners Nursing and Technology (BONENT), the National Nephrology Certification Organization (NNCO), and/or the The Nephrology Nursing Certification Commission (NNCC). While certification is often voluntary, taking the time to gain certification helps establish you as a skilled professional and can often lead to more responsibility and better pay.

NOTES FROM THE FIELD

Certified hemodialysis technician (CHT), Biomedical technician, *Toms River, New Jersey*

Q: *How did you get your job?*

A: About 10 years ago I was an EMT [emergency medical technician]. I had a friend who was an educator at a hospital. She knew my heart was in helping people, so she asked me if I would be interested in becoming a technician. I was a sponge, wanting to learn everything. Wherever there was a seminar, I would go.

Two years ago, I was promoted to bio-med technician. I've run the gamut: I went from technician to patient care to repairing machines. The only thing I haven't done yet is manage the facility.

Q: *What do you like best about your job?*

A: For me, there's versatility. I don't come in and do one thing all day long. I need to be challenged, and there are a lot of challenges in dialysis. I love the patients. I love talking with them. I love being able to fix things. If something has gone wrong, there's a challenge to figure it out so that the rest of the day goes fine. That's what I love about it; there's always something going on.

Q: *What's the most challenging part of your job?*

A: It's a tough job because you're taking care of sick patients. You see those same sick patients every single week, three times a week for years. It's very hard to watch someone you've taken care of for years diminish.

Q: *What are the keys to success to being a dialysis technician?*

A: The first thing is to get certified. When you have that certificate, it says you know what you're doing. You've gone through the courses. You've kept taking courses to keep up with your certification. Also, you work long days. You're on your feet all day. If you don't love what you're doing, there's no sense doing it.

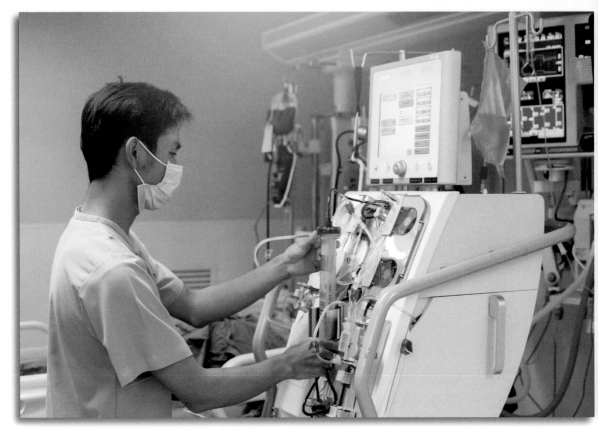

▲ Dialysis technician training teaches students about kidney function, how to properly set up and operate machines and insert needles.

Learn the Lingo

Here are a few words to know as a dialysis technician:

- **BONENT** Shorthand for the Board of Nephrology Examiners Nursing and Technology, a professional organization that certifies people to work as dialysis technicians.

- **Patient care technician (PCT)** A dialysis technician who specializes in caring for patients while they receive treatment.

- **Hemodialysis** The most popular form of dialysis. During the treatment, a patient's blood is drained into a machine with two sections. The blood goes into one side of the machine; the particles of waste in the blood go into the other side, which contains a fluid called dialysate. A thin membrane separates the two sides. As the blood goes through the machine, the waste in the blood goes through the microscopic holes in the membrane and is washed away in the dialysate. The blood cells, which are too big to go through the membrane, are sent back to the body.

- **Nephrology** The branch of internal medicine dealing with the study of the function and diseases of the kidney.

Finding a Job

Contact a hospital or medical clinic that provides dialysis treatment. Many centers provide on-the-job training to qualified high school applicants. At the very least, they may be able to recommend schools that offer dialysis technician programs. After completing your training, you'll receive a certificate or technical diploma in your field that shows employers that you've received the proper training. Your school can also often help you find a job in your chosen field.

You can also check with employment agencies that specialize in medical careers. If you're interested in working in a Veterans Affairs (VA) hospital, you should reach out to the U.S. Office of Personnel Management.

You might also try checking with professional and medical associations that specialize in dialysis treatments. Two good bets include the National Kidney Foundation and the National Association of Nephrology Technicians/Technologists.

Tips for Success

- Learn as much as you can on the job. There's no better training than on-the-job practice and observing other professionals.

- Enroll in seminars sponsored by professional organizations in your field. These associations offer valuable training. Also, take the time to gain certification in your field: doing so will often lead to more opportunities and better pay.

Reality Check

Be very, very careful. Because dialysis technicians work with blood, they must use extra care not to spread infectious diseases. To keep you and your patients safe, you must follow strict sterilization guidelines and wear protective gowns, gloves, and face shields.

Related Jobs to Consider

Cardiovascular technologist. If you're a whiz with computers and electronics, you might want to consider a career as a cardiovascular technologist. As a cardiovascular technologist, you measure, analyze, and take images of the heart and circulatory system. These tests help physicians see if a patient has heart disease, and if so, how extensive it is.

Clinical laboratory technician. If you enjoy doing lab experiments in science class, you might enjoy working as a clinical laboratory technician in a medical lab. As a clinical laboratory technician, you prepare lab specimens, perform manual tests on the specimens, and operate automated analyzers.

LEARN MORE ONLINE

BOARD OF NEPHROLOGY EXAMINERS NURSING AND TECHNOLOGY
This organization specializes in the certification of nephrology professionals. http://www.bonent.org

NATIONAL ASSOCIATION OF NEPHROLOGY TECHNICIANS/TECHNOLOGISTS
This is the organization for nephrology professionals. http://www.nant.biz

NEPHROLOGY NURSING CERTIFICATION COMMISSION
This site provides info on nephrology nursing and certification. http://www.nncc-exam.org

NATIONAL KIDNEY FOUNDATION
A health organization dedicated to preventing kidney disease. http://www.kidney.org

How to Move Up

- Become a chief technologist. These professionals supervise the work of the dialysis technicians.

- Look into surgical technician career. These technicians assist doctors and nurses during surgery.

- Build strong organizational and computer skills. Advanced skills can lead to a job as a hospital unit secretary or unit support associate.

- Become a registered nurse (RN). To become an RN, you'll need a two-year associate's degree or a four-year bachelor's degree. Registered nurses have more responsibility and can work their way into supervisory positions.

TEXT-DEPENDENT QUESTIONS

1. *What is the purpose of dialysis?*

2. *What kind of training is needed for this job?*

3. *How do you get certified?*

4. *What is hemodialysis?*

RESEARCH PROJECTS

1. *The first step toward working in the dialysis field is understanding how and why healthy kidneys do what they do. Where are kidneys in the body? Why are kidneys important for health? What types of problems can develop? Look for answers at the National Institutes of Health (https://www.niddk.nih.gov/health-information/kidney-disease/kidneys-how-they-work).*

2. *Find out more about kidney disease. What causes it? Are certain types of people more likely to develop it than others? What kinds of treatments are available and what are the side effects? Start your search for answers at the National Kidney Foundation's site (https://www.kidney.org/kidneydisease).*

Nursing Assistant

8

Discover the field of medicine. Learn indispensable skills. Be where people need you most.

WORDS TO UNDERSTAND

arduous: physically difficult and tiring.
hospices: homes for the care of terminally ill patients.
vital signs: measurements of basic body functions: blood pressure, pulse, body temperature, and breathing.

Looking for work where you can really make a difference in someone's life? Want a job where you'll be known and appreciated? Consider a position as a nursing assistant. Nursing assistants are the foot soldiers of the booming health care industry. They provide direct care services at hospitals, nursing homes, and other care facilities. Today there are well over 1.5 million nursing assistants, and new positions are opening daily. That's because the baby boomers are aging and medical advances mean that older people are living longer. What's more, growing numbers of the elderly are choosing to live in long-term health care facilities. All of this means that, with training ranging from a couple of weeks to several months, you can step into this new career right away.

▲ A nursing assistant helps his patient get some exercise outdoors.

Is This Job Right for You?

To find out if being a nursing assistant is a good fit for you, read each of the following questions and answer "Yes" or "No."

Yes	*No*	**1.**	*Do you like helping people?*
Yes	*No*	**2.**	*Do you have a friendly, caring manner?*
Yes	*No*	**3.**	*Do you have good stamina, and can you be on your feet for hours?*
Yes	*No*	**4.**	*Are you strong enough to lift 50 pounds?*
Yes	*No*	**5.**	*Would you be comfortable taking care of someone's physical needs?*
Yes	*No*	**6.**	*Do you work well with others?*
Yes	*No*	**7.**	*Are you responsible and dependable?*
Yes	*No*	**8.**	*Do you take direction well?*
Yes	*No*	**9.**	*Are you sensitive to the needs of other people?*
Yes	*No*	**10.**	*Are you patient, and can you keep your emotions in check?*

If you answered "Yes" to most of these questions, consider a career as a nursing assistant. To find out more about this job, read on.

What's the Work Like?

As a nursing assistant, you'll provide people who are ill, elderly, or disabled with their basic human needs. You'll help these patients and seniors with eating, walking, grooming, bathing, dressing, even relieving themselves. All the while, you'll help them keep a sense of dignity and privacy. You will also observe and report on your patients' or residents' physical and mental well-being. You may use medical equipment, such as blood-pressure cuffs, to check patients' **vital signs**. You may be asked to read the gauges and dials on their monitors and hook up equipment. You'll also be the one to deliver messages or answer patients' call lights, signaling that they need help. You'll

> ## TALKING MONEY
>
> Nursing assistants earn an average of $26,590 per year, according to the U.S. Bureau of Labor Statistics. Those who work for the government and in private hospitals tend to make the most, while those who work in assisted living facilities often make the least.

help nurses with other tasks, including moving equipment and transporting and lifting patients. When patients or residents become confused, angry, frustrated, or fearful, you may be called upon to soothe or even restrain them. Because you'll have day-to-day contact, especially if you work in a nursing home, you may develop close relationships with the people you care for. They may come to depend on you for comfort and companionship. You may even become among their closest connections.

The work can be **arduous**, so you'll need to be physically fit. Nursing assistants should be able to lift at least 50 pounds. You'll also need to take direction well, follow the rules of

▲ Although the biggest growth area in the field is caring for the elderly, nursing assistants are also needed to care for children and young adults.

your institution and understand what all patients' rights are. The job is hugely rewarding. You really get to know individuals in a very close way. You'll share laughs and concerns, and your patients' appreciation will be a huge job bonus.

Who's Hiring?

- Nursing homes or other long-term care facilities

- Public, private, or federal hospitals, such as veterans' hospitals

- Rehabilitation facilities, which help people recover from disabilities such as strokes or auto accidents

- **Hospices**

- Outpatient care facilities and senior centers

- Agencies that provide temporary help to ease staffing shortages

- Private for-profit institutions, which are both cost-conscious and geared toward delivering quality care

- Public institutions, including prison hospitals

Where Are the Jobs?

Your job environment will vary depending on what type of employer you choose. If you work in a hospital, chances are that you may work on the general medical-surgical floor. Other areas of hospitals, such as the mother-baby floors and pediatric floors, also require nursing assistants, but jobs in these departments are popular and may be hard to land—at least right away.

In a nursing home or other care facility, your environment will be shaped by the rules and conditions, the institution and your supervisors put in place. Staffing levels will play a huge role in your overall job satisfaction and the quality of the job environment. A typical nursing assistant to patient ratio in a nursing home is about 8 to 14 patients per assistant: The lower, of course, the better. U.S. standards suggest that nursing assistants should be able to give each patient more than an hour of individual care per day.

The shift you take—daytime, evening, or night—will also affect your job environment. Daytime is usually the busiest shift because patients get their procedures done. Aides on the second shift also have a heavy workload. However, some young nursing assistants prefer this shift because they have time to themselves during the day. Then,

TALKING TRENDS

Nursing assistants are in big demand. By 2024, expect to see more than 325,000 new positions. In fact, in 2006, nursing assistants were among the 25 fastest growing jobs.

when their shift ends, usually around 10:30 p.m., it's still not too late to catch up with friends—especially on the weekends. Nights are the quietest shift. The downside is, of course, that you're up all night. Nursing assistants who work nights and evenings may earn slightly more pay per hour.

Which type of employer should you choose? That depends on your personality. Some nursing assistants consider hospital work more prestigious. However, it's very demanding work, and patients move on and off of the floors far faster. They're also often sicker. This can mean less time to interact with them. In nursing homes and long-term care facilities, there's more opportunity for one-on-one interaction with patients. However, nursing assistants are often called upon to do a broader range of tasks. As you choose your employer, consider its reputation for treatment of patients, as well as its employees. Look for an employer who offers employee benefits.

A Typical Day

Here are the highlights of a typical evening shift at a nursing home.

See what it's like to be a nursing assistant.

Check your patients. Shifts often start with nursing assistants making their rounds. This means going from patient to patient, seeing if their "call light" is on, and checking on their physical condition. This might include, for instance, making sure elderly patients are dry.

Assist during mealtime. Haul and pass out trays of food, assist certain residents, for instance, by spoon-feeding them or helping them handle a straw. Help nurses pass out the patients' medications.

Ready patients for bed. Pass out snacks. Give showers and help these patients dress for bed. Put residents to bed, and chart each patient's activities for daily living (ADLs) in the proper books.

Start Preparing Now

- Look for a vocational-education course or program in health careers at your high school.

- Take science classes like biology to help you better understand how the body works.

- Volunteer at a hospital or long-term care facility.

Training and How to Get It

In some states, you need to have a high school diploma or a credential of general educational development (GED) to get a job as a nursing assistant. In other states, you don't need a diploma or GED, though it's preferred. To check your state's requirements, you'll need to contact your state's agency that covers nursing assistant training programs. Links to state pages can be found on the Web site of the National Network of Career Nursing Assistants: http://www.cna-network.org. The human resources departments of many hospitals and nursing homes can also refer you.

In order to work in a long-term care facility, you'll have to become certified. This means you'll have to have some training and pass your state's nursing assistant exam. The amount of training varies by state; it could be anywhere between 75 and 150 hours. To become certified, you'll probably also need to pass a drug test and have a clean criminal record.

During your nursing assistant training, you'll learn the basics of patient care, including vital signs, nutrition, symptoms of patient distress, infection control, weights and measures, and basic emergency procedures. You may be given training in the management of death and dying. You'll learn good communication skills and conflict resolution.

To get your training, check with health care facilities in your area. Many offer classes that are free or even paid, especially if you agree to work at that facility. Training usually lasts

NOTES FROM THE FIELD

Nursing assistant, Amherst, Virginia

Q: *How did you get your job?*

A: I started with a six-week training course through Virginia Baptist and Central Health. As part of our training, I did my clinical work at Fairmont Crossing Assisted Living Facility, and I got hired there. I also passed the certified nurse assistant licensing exam. Getting the license gives you an edge, and it helps you get the job you want, rather than just coming in off the street and trying to get hired. I've been on the job for eight months now.

Q: *What do you like best about your job?*

A: I like using the medical equipment, like taking the patient's blood pressure and respiration rate. I also like my teammates—the other certified nurse assistants and the nurses. We have a good team here. I also like getting to know the residents. I've gotten to know all 30 people on my floor. They're really nice.

Q: *What's the most challenging part of your job?*

A: It can get stressful at times, and you have to learn to deal with this. Also, some of the residents don't know what they're saying or doing. You have to be patient and get to know the different personalities.

Q: *What are the keys to success to being a nursing assistant?*

A: You have to have a good attitude and recognize that your patients are human. They have rights. You also have to learn to abide by certain rules. It helps to have a good work ethic and be willing to help your teammates out. I've changed since I've started working here. I understand more about people now.

between two and six weeks. You can also get training by taking a course offered at a local community college or through your Red Cross. These classes usually last between three and six months. Training includes classroom time and time working directly with patients. You

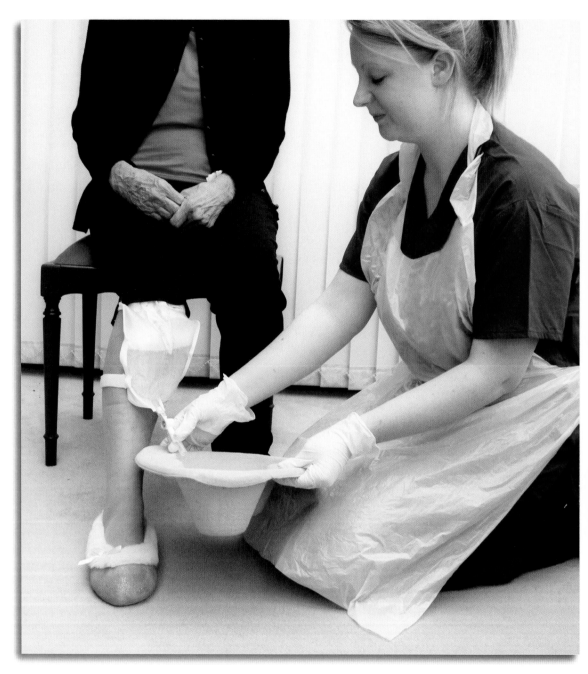

▲ Although the job is fulfilling, a nursing assistant's tasks are not always pleasant. Here, a nursing assistant empties the urine bag of a patient in a nursing home.

need both class time and clinical time to get certified. If you see nursing assistant training offered online, beware. Online classes won't include the one-to-one patient training that you need to get certified.

Learn the Lingo

Here are a few words you'll hear as a nursing assistant:

- **ADL care** Care that's related to a patient's *activities for daily living* (ADLs). This is what most nursing assistants are responsible for.

- **CNA registry** A list of *certified nursing assistants*. By law, each state has a registry of all nursing assistants who pass their state's exam.

- **Vital signs** These are the signs of life of a person. They include body temperature, pulse rate, respiration rate, and often blood pressure.

Finding a Job

To find a job, simply contact a care facility that you think you'd like to work for. Present yourself as dependable, trustworthy, responsible, respectful, and caring. If you're certified, you'll put yourself ahead of the pack. If you're not certified, don't worry. Many facilities offer training and will help you get certified. Others, such as hospitals, don't require this. You'll also have a better chance of being employed if you're available for any shift—days, evenings, or nights. If a job isn't open when you check at first, be persistent. This career area has a high turnover rate. New positions open up frequently, so don't give up. Check back every few weeks or months to see if an opening has become available.

Tips for Success

- Keep your sense of humor. Always keep your cool and back away from a confrontation. If you respond to a patient in anger, you could lose your job.

- Your time as a nursing assistant can be invaluable for research to discover which health care specialties professionally interest you.

▲ Nursing assistants spend a lot of time with their patients. It's important for them to be polite and understanding of their patients' discomfort and stress.

Reality Check

Watch your back! When it comes to nursing assistants, take this advice to heart. On-the-job back injuries are surprisingly common, so use special equipment and seek help from others when lifting or transferring patients.

Related Jobs to Consider

Home health aide. Home health aides perform tasks that are similar to nursing assistants. The difference is that home health aides work directly in the home. Home health aides tend to form close bonds with their patients.

Psychiatric aide. Psychiatric aides are similar to nursing assistants, except that they work in mental health facilities or psychiatric wards. They often do more work restraining unruly patients.

How to Move Up

- Become a physical therapy technician, surgical technician, or laboratory technician.

- Become a hospital unit secretary or a unit support associate if you have strong computer skills.

- Become a licensed practical nurse (LPN). To become an LPN, you'll need 12 months of training in basic nursing skills. You'll also need to pass a national exam. LPNs can administer most medications, change dressings, and perform other technical skills.

- Become a registered nurse (RN). To become an RN, you'll need a two-year associate's degree or a four-year bachelor's degree. Registered nurses, especially those with four-year degrees, are qualified to move into supervisory positions.

LEARN MORE ONLINE

NURSING ASSISTANT GUIDES
This site includes frequently asked questions and information about getting certified. https://nursingassistantguides.com/

NATIONAL ASSOCIATION OF HEALTH CARE ASSISTANTS
With a membership of more than 26,000 nursing assistants, this group offers a yearly convention, a magazine, a message board, and job listings. http://www.nahcacares.org

TEXT-DEPENDENT QUESTIONS

1. *What types of firms and organizations hire nursing assistants?*

2. *What is a typical day like?*

3. *How do you get trained in this field?*

4. *How do you find a job?*

RESEARCH PROJECTS

1. *Find out if you'd like working with elderly, sick, or needy people by volunteering at your community hospital or a nearby nursing home.*

2. *Find out more about getting certified. Read about the certified nursing assistant (CNA) exam and try some sample questions here: https://nursingassistantguides. com/guide-to-studying-for-and-taking-the-cna-exam-certified-nursing-assistant-test/.*

▲ Home health care, particularly for older people, is a strong area of employment.

INDEX

preparation 9
  dental assistant 31–32
  dialysis technician 92
  dispensing optician 41, 43
  emergency medical technician/
    paramedic 80
  medical receptionist 53
  nursing assistant 104
  occupational therapist aide/physical therapy
    aide 19–21
  veterinary assistant/laboratory animal
    caretaker 67

promotion
  dental assistant 34
  dialysis technician 96
  dispensing optician 45–46
  emergency medical technician/paramedic 84
  medical receptionist 58
  nursing assistant 109
  occupational therapist aide/physical therapy
    aide 22
  veterinary assistant/laboratory animal
    caretaker 70

salary
  dental assistant 26
  dialysis technician 89
  dispensing optician 38
  emergency medical technician/paramedic 75
  medical receptionist 50
  nursing assistant 100
  occupational therapist aide/physical therapy
    aide 15
  veterinary assistant/laboratory animal
    caretaker 63

training 6–7, 10
  dental assistant 31, 34
  dialysis technician 92, 95
  dispensing optician 42, 45
  emergency medical technician/paramedic
    80–81, 84
  medical receptionist 54–55
  nursing assistant 99, 104–105, 107
  occupational therapist aide/physical therapy
    aide 20, 22
  veterinary assistant/laboratory animal
    caretaker 67

trends
  dental assistant 28
  dialysis technician 90
  dispensing optician 41
  emergency medical technician/paramedic 77
  medical receptionist 53
  nursing assistant 103
  occupational therapist aide/physical therapy
    aide 16
  veterinary assistant/laboratory animal
    caretaker 64

work environment
  dental assistant 28
  dialysis technician 90
  dispensing optician 40
  emergency medical technician/paramedic 77
  medical receptionist 52–53
  nursing assistant 102–103
  occupational therapist aide/physical therapy
    aide 16–17
  veterinary assistant/laboratory animal
    caretaker 65

PHOTO CREDITS